CORE
CONNECTION FOR
RIDER & HORSE

For Ruth
with very best wishes
Lindsay Wilcox-Reid

CORE
CONNECTION FOR
RIDER & HORSE

Preparing Body and Mind
for Riding Performance in Partnership

Lindsay Wilcox-Reid

J.A. ALLEN · LONDON

First published in 2013 by
J.A. Allen
Clerkenwell House
Clerkenwell Green
London EC1R 0HT
www.allenbooks.co.uk

J.A. Allen is an imprint of Robert Hale Limited

ISBN 978-1-908809-09-4

A catalogue record for this book is available from the British Library

Edited by Martin Diggle
Designed and typeset by Paul Saunders
Photographs by Bob Atkins (except page 204 (top), by HoofPrints Photography)
Illustrations on pages 16, 32, 142, 193, 196, 197 and 205 by Jennifer Bell
Illustrations on pages 30, 42, 48, 49, 50 and 51 by Lisa Brooke
Illustrations on pages 22, 28, 91, 99 and 101 by Carole Vincer
Printed in Singapore by Craft Print International Limited

Disclaimer of Liability

The author and publisher shall have neither liability nor responsibility to any person or entity with respect to any loss or damage caused or alleged to be caused directly or indirectly by the information contained in this book. While the book is as accurate as the author can make it, there may be errors, omissions, and inaccuracies.

For Alf; my partner and my friend.

Got any sweets?

Contents

Foreword

During 2011, for the first time in England, the *École de Légèreté* (School of Lightness) instructor training commenced under my directorship. Since then, Lindsay Wilcox-Reid has been an enthusiastic follower of the principles of the school, attending all the theoretical and practical courses. Although I have not known her for long, it was nevertheless with pleasure that I accepted the invitation to write the foreword to this book, for two major reasons:

Lindsay is an established and widely recognised professional rider and trainer. However, faced with the perverse effects that can arise from the dogmas of official dressage, she has long since undertaken to reform her riding and her teaching in depth. I have great respect for this lucidity and courage – to paraphrase Shakespeare's *Hamlet*: 'There are customs that it is more honourable to breach than to follow.'

In addition to the remarkable chapters in this book on physical and mental education of the rider, Lindsay shows that she has already assimilated the principles, methods and processes of our school for the basic training of the horse – this, despite unfortunately having been unable to attend our inaugural mounted course. She will therefore obtain her rightful place in our next promotional course for instructors – on a horse this time.

To conclude, I cannot recommend this book enough to all those with a passion for riding who are looking for a philosophy that is both effective and respectful of the horse, because it is based on a deep understanding of his nature and biological needs.

With my best wishes for a wide readership.

PHILIPPE KARL

Acknowledgements

It is with huge appreciation and gratitude that I must thank the following people for being instrumental in facilitating the writing of this book, in one way or another.

Chris, Oliver and George: thank you for your patience with my being shut away typing in a room for hours on end.

Mum, thank you for the contribution of your amazing chapter and for your encouragement of my passion for horses and for learning.

Dennis, thank you for your appreciation of my efforts and continued support – Bruno sends a kiss.

Dad and Vanessa, thank you for supporting and enabling a remarkable shift in my understanding.

Emma Stamenkovic: the list is too long to specify, so I'll thank you for all-round life support!

Lisa Brooke, thank you for being a fantastic friend and giving so much time and expertise to help me.

Bob Atkins, thank you for cracking pictures once again.

Sally Elliott, thank you for your modelling skills and your enthusiasm; it is wonderful to see you and Lottie grow together into a fabulous partnership.

I must express my gratitude to Black Country Saddles for supplying me with such amazing kit which makes developing a correct position and communication with the horse so much easier. Thank you also to matchydressage.com for dressing my horses so impeccably, to Sally Cartwright of Saddlery Services for being so supportive and being my saddle-adviser and fitter extraordinaire. Thanks also to Bliss Bedding for supplying the team with comfortable bedrooms!

Lisa Ashton, thank you so much for your valuable input and encouragement on the response work, and thanks to Dr Andrew McLean for fantastic foundation integration.

Martin Haines and Anthony Fletcher of Intelligent Training Systems; massive thanks for blowing my mind! Riding and coaching will never be the same again.

Mickey Gavin, thank you for opening my eyes that little bit wider and giving me new tools for developing deeper relationships with my horses.

Liz Oakenfold, thank you for your skills, perception and intuition. You are a true friend and you know not the keys you have given me!

Lesley Gowers, thank you for giving me another opportunity to empty my head of most of the thoughts that swirl around in it, and for allowing me to include so many extra words!

Thank you to my clients, teachers and the various people in my life who continue to drive my search for knowledge and an enlightened level of skill.

And finally, a huge thank you from me and my horses to Philippe Karl for sharing his vision and wisdom in how we can learn to dance.

Thank you to my horses; you are my teachers and my friends.

For more information about Lindsay Wilcox-Reid
and Equipilates™ tuition, please visit
www.equipilates.com

Introduction

The perfect performance, whether that to you is an enjoyable hack, a confident cross-country round or a winning international dressage test, relies on clear communication between horse and rider. We can maximise the effectiveness of our communication by exploring the factors that are influential to that performance. This book will explore how and why these factors impact on our riding success, and by understanding and taking ownership of their influence, we can optimise both performance and partnership. Riding well requires competence in so many areas – we will discuss some of those here, and plan strategies for improving your ability in each one. You need the ability to follow your horse's movement (which requires that your body's shock-absorption capacity is as efficient as possible) and the ability to influence your horse's balance effectively and with respect to his nature and structure. This means being able to use your body in a very organised, precise way, which is always consistent – really talented riders who seem able to get any horse going sweetly possess a great sense of timing of the application of their aids, and also – perhaps even more importantly – the cessation of their aids. You need an awareness of the complexity of the challenges you are presenting to your horse, and to know how to break these down into achievable parts. You need an understanding of the physical capabilities of *your* horse so that you can help him to discover new feelings of balance and relaxation, and to enhance his suppleness and strength. You need the ability to be an effective trainer and so instil confidence in your horse, and the theoretical understanding of what you are trying to achieve so that you can plan a sensible programme of progression – and the ability to keep a sense of perspective (and a sense of humour!) when things don't go to plan.

Every time you ride your horse you are setting up patterns of thought, patterns of movement, and patterns of future posture not only with your own body but with that of your horse as well. In fact, when approached with care and thought, the work that you do with him can be immensely beneficial to his mind and body and can help to make him more balanced, more flexible, stronger, eager, willing, and a delight to ride. Specific exercises, giving consideration to where your horse has weaknesses (where he finds things particularly hard) and also to where things feel easier, can seriously improve posture, performance and long-term prospects of soundness. However, just as the right work at the right time with the right approach can be educational on so many levels, overloading the horse's mind with confusing signals and his body with inappropriate weight distribution, poor balance, and ill-chosen exercises can compound problems he may already have – and can certainly create new ones! By clarifying communication between the two of you and experimenting with useful exercises that can provide information and feedback about which areas you and your horse would benefit from working on, you can build a better partnership on the ground, in the saddle, and in the competition arena.

Note

It is of the utmost importance that you are aware that your horse can present subtle or clear difficulties in ridden performance, groundwork or behaviour if he is in discomfort. Spooking, shying, bucking, bolting and rearing, reluctance to work, reluctance to stop, or difficulties in performing the movements you ask of your horse are very often indicators of pain or restriction and therefore it is imperative that you consult a skilled physical therapist or vet to assess and treat your horse if necessary. Useful links for relevant associations to contact are included in the Recommended Reading list at the back of this book. Of course, any issue that you may be having with your riding could also arise from lack of physical preparation for the demand (the horse's structure isn't strong enough) or perhaps you are inadvertently making it problematical for the horse through being in an unhelpful balance or not asking clearly enough, or asking in a way that is beyond the horse's current comprehension.

My journey so far has presented me and the riders and horses with whom I work, with (amongst others) the training challenges presented and explored herein. Developing equestrian skills is a lifelong journey, and therefore my perspective naturally grows along the way to include new questions, different answers and all the experience that is related to those challenges. I have learned to find new strategies for dealing with issues which were at the very limit of, and sometimes beyond, my skill level at the time I first encountered them. I have been extremely fortunate to meet some incredibly skilled and talented people along the way thus far, who have had truly massive impact on my horsy world, and have been instrumental in causing a major paradigm shift. I really hope that you find this book offers thought-provoking ideas to help you discover new sensations and perhaps new solutions. A life with horses is certainly a rollercoaster of a journey, with tears, laughter; denial and realisation; frustration, inspiration and elation! I can't think of a more wonderful one – can you?

CHAPTER ONE

Riding in Partnership – the Connections Within

How many factors are involved in a successful partnership between horse and rider? That partnership might mean enjoying a leisurely hack on a Sunday afternoon; spook free, in control, perhaps with some high-speed work for the adrenalin junkie – or maybe at a steady walk for the rider requiring relaxation, with horse and rider simply enjoying their time together. Could it mean a dressage test, perfectly executed, with exactly the right amount of pizzazz and poise – relaxed yet raring to go; a balletic expression of the gymnastic capabilities of the horse's most athletic movements? Could it mean jumping with such precision and power that the horse appears to have springs in his feet? Perhaps it describes the horse who responds to the lightest touch of the rider's leg – the slightest change of balance or tone in their seat – the merest whisper of a feel on the rein. A horse who breathes, thinks – *chooses* – to act upon the rider's every whim with joy and grace. This horse might also be capable of doing all of the above tasks too – but it is surely the horse whom every rider would choose as a partner. The good news is that it is perfectly possible to train *your* horse to be more responsive in every way, and to improve your influence as a rider beyond recognition. Becoming aware of the connections in our own bodies – the biomechanical connections, the connections between our aims and actions, the connections between our minds and bodies – and of similar connections within our horse, helps us connect more fully with him. A deep, trusting and consistent connection can be developed from the centre of one being to the centre of another: a true core connection.

Let's look at the factors involved in building the perfect performance and, within each aspect, how you can start achieving your goals, with real, achievable, measurable steps *today*. The following chapters will explore each factor in detail.

Rider alignment – how your body *looks* (your 'form') and how your body actually *works* inside biomechanically (how you 'function': the workings of your joints, muscles and nerves) – determines how you sit on your horse, how well your body can absorb the shock of his movement without strain and how well you can stay balanced whilst resisting any unwanted movement forces being exerted (like a spook or buck). It also determines how well you can apply aids to your horse, and also cease them when they aren't needed anymore.

Another matter of fundamental importance is highlighted by the question 'Where is the weight?' Whenever you get on your horse, you are giving him messages about how to stand and how to move, simply through how your weight is positioned on his back – this means that really your alignment can be your most powerful ally, or your most frustrating adversary! Generally speaking, your horse will always try to adjust his balance so that your weight is concentrated right in the middle of his back (just as you would shrug an odd-shaped or unevenly loaded backpack into the centre of yours); this makes it easier for him to carry you. However, in order to do this, he might have to recruit many compensatory mechanisms (bracing certain bits of himself) in order to balance and do what you are asking of him as well. Over time, this can cause chronic stress on his structure – certainly muscle soreness, tightness, restriction in flexibility and joint function and possibly even lameness as particular soft tissues take too much strain, and certain bony structures are subjected to too much compressive force. It is important that, as a rider, you are aware of the influence of your weight and how it can assist you in training your horse in harmony. Your weight can be either *in balance* with your horse (harmonising) or in a *different balance*, which has the effect of displacing the horse. A lot of riders are unintentionally displacing their horses all the time and are never in a useful balance, or harmonising with the horse (which gives him a release of pressure and therefore a reward). However, if we use our weight consciously and are aware of where 'neutral' is, we can displace the horse on purpose to make changes to his balance, for example turning, moving laterally, increasing forward motion or the loading of his hindquarters.

On the other hand, if there is restriction present in your body, it is difficult to use weight aids with any precision, as there will always be one side of you that is easier to load than the other. Your body will probably already be loading in one direction without you even knowing it. For this reason it is really helpful to experiment with the Swiss ball exercises in Chapter 6 to give you an idea of the movements you find easier, and which ones seem harder. This will be linked to your intrinsic biomechanics and later we'll explore why you find it easier to perform certain movements and not others. We'll also look at ways to use weight aids to influence your horse's balance later on in Chapter 10.

In my book *Pilates for Riders*, I explored a 'stack of boxes' concept, which I'll reproduce briefly here. Imagine your body is a basic stack of three boxes: your pelvic box, your ribcage box and your head box on top. All of these boxes can tilt forwards and back, tilt left or right, shift left or right, shift forwards or back, and rotate left or right. When all of the boxes are stacked neatly one on top of another, without tilts, shifts or rotations, we term this 'neutral spine'. Much of the asymmetry, and many of the unhelpful postural patterns we display, actually represent patterns that we have formed or developed through something physical, or emotional (or both!) getting stuck somewhere. In Chapter 11 you'll learn more about how the power of the mind has a massive effect on the body. Physical trauma can of course have a massive impact on how well, or not, our bodies work for us, but so does emotional trauma, whether sudden shock or loss, or the more insidious 'drip, drip, drip …' feed of worries, which leaves us suffering from chronic stress. This can give us very real and very significant discomfort, which can manifest itself in such a variety of ways. When we release and unwind unnecessary tensions, the body's true alignment starts to reveal itself. In *Pilates for Riders* I mentioned a chap called Phil Greenfield who is a very gifted body worker and an intuitive sort of person. He comes out with all sorts of little gems; one I particularly remember was 'If all the people who had physical problems had psychological therapy, and all those with psychological problems had physical therapy, everyone in the world would be fine!' Obviously rather tongue-in-cheek, but worth a thought! So, what could it be that 'gets stuck' and why? How can we 'unstick' it, and help it stay that way?

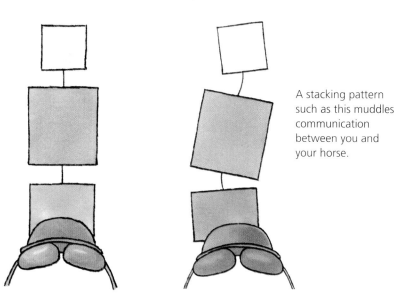

Having your boxes stacked correctly in a neutral alignment means that the channels of communication between your and your horse's bodies are clear. It also means you are a more organised 'load'.

A stacking pattern such as this muddles communication between you and your horse.

The rider in the accompanying photo finds rotating to the right more difficult; by peering directly down her spine can you see how, in relation to her 'pelvic box', her ribcage box is stuck in a turn to the left? Any movement which requires her to rotate right is trickier for her, for example turning on circles right, shoulder-in right, half-pass right, pirouettes right. When there is a rotation pattern presenting like this (we have very slightly exaggerated it for the photograph) it is often linked to left-right imbalances too.

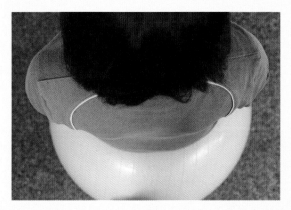

For example, the more Sally's body goes into the left rotation, which it does when she's learning something new, difficult, or her horse is very lively (more about this later!), the more her body shortens on the left and tends to displace her weight to the right. This gives the horse a weight aid right, which is most unhelpful because her horse, Lottie, has a postural pattern that also drifts right. If your body is really stuck in one particular 'stacking pattern' (and this could result from a culmination of injury, postural habits or any number of seemingly insignificant tweaks from years ago), movements on the horse that require your body to assume a different stacking pattern will prove difficult. For example, if, in the saddle your pelvic box is really rotated to the left you may find difficulties in the flying change; in the change right to left, despite the aim of keeping your upper body relatively still, the movement of the horse's left lateral pair of legs to jump through onto the new lead requires the ability of your left hip to be taken forward with the horse's motion. If your left hip is restricted in coming forward, it may well block, or at least reduce, the expression in the change, or perhaps your body will compensate instead by displacing sideways. In any case, there could either be no change, a struggle to change or one which lacks straightness.

In Chapter 4 we'll explore a series of exercises which take your body through the various different combinations of stacking patterns and movements of the 'boxes'. These help to unwind your body and raise your awareness of where you would benefit from playing with different movements. If any position of any box is possible, your body finding alignment somewhere in the middle should become progressively easier.

When we're thinking about the alignment and weight distribution of the rider, we also need to consider how the body's mechanics are actually working, as they affect how movement forces are dealt with by the body – your shock-absorption capacity. If there are restrictions in how well your joints are able to follow and manage all the oscillations of the horse's back, sitting to each gait will be tricky. If one side of your pelvis and hip joint is 'stuck', or both sides are stuck but one more so than the other, this will influence completely your entire position, from how well you can ask for a walk transition from halt, to how well you can sit the trot, to whether you sit with a round back, or a hollow back. Pelvic restriction also means that the efficiency of your core muscles will be compromised.

Form versus function

Your 'form' is how you look to your trainer or other observers and how your weight appears to be distributed in the saddle; where your legs hang, whether you're in neutral spine, the angles of your joints, how your shoulders are positioned, etc. This is called 'extrinsic biomechanics', which also refers to the study or analysis of performing movements or tasks in the most mechanically efficient way. Movement analysis, including visually assessing your position and riding, is working with your extrinsic biomechanics. In this age of complex technological advances, there is software available that can capture measurements of joint angles, pressure sensors and a variety of scientifically useful devices, and there are experts specialising in interpreting and making sense of the data readings. Our top-class competitors have regular access to this type of support to monitor gait patterns and loading in order to maximise performance potential.

Your 'function' refers to how your body is actually working (or not!) on the inside – the behaviour of your muscles, nerves and joints. Your horse can feel which areas within your body are working properly to absorb his movement, and which aren't, which results in blocking it. These 'inside workings' are known as 'intrinsic biomechanics'.

Two people could present with extremely similar postural patterns, or 'forms' and yet the areas in their bodies which are actually restricted (their intrinsic biomechanics) could be totally different. Having good form is an important half of the mechanical requirements of riding – this is what we are taught to develop almost from the moment we start riding; the ear, shoulder, hip, heel line which is the classic neutral spine. However, although it is an important half, it is just that; half the story. The 'function' bit is really the missing link in so much of what is taught today to improve rider posture and position.

Often, when a rider's position is corrected, it has a really positive effect straight away. This is great, because the horse will always provide feedback, even if it is subtle, when there has been an improvement made in how the rider is using their body. This doesn't just mean how they are aligned or how their weight is distributed, but how they actually use their body to give aids or signals to the horse. Improving 'form' will make a positive impact in terms of packaging up the rider's body into a more organised load for the horse to carry; it will look better, and in

Right: When we look at 'form' in a rider, we're looking for neutral spine; for the diagonal lines to be equal and the cross point to be in the middle. We are also looking for the diagonal lines which run from front to back to be equal, with the cross point in the middle. The lines at the sides of the body should be parallel and of an equal length, and the lines going across the body should be horizontal.

Above left: This is my friend Lisa, who is also demonstrating the reflexes in Chapter 8. The photo is reproduced from *Pilates for Riders*, so you might recognise it if you've read that book. At nearly six feet tall she has always had good 'form' on a horse and, as you can see, looks very elegant. However, she has had certain issues within her body which have restricted her from making progress in the past. You wouldn't know to look at her (unless you looked closely!), but her horse would tell her when there was a problem. Even someone like Lisa, who has pretty much a 'textbook' position, can restrict the flow of her horse's movement when her muscles, nerves and joints aren't operating properly. The trouble is, unless she had an intrinsic biomechanical assessment, she wouldn't necessarily be aware of this until it got to the point where she was in discomfort.

improving how the boxes are stacked, will probably allow aids to be applied and transmitted more clearly.

Sometimes though, you can be trying to achieve something different; a different leg position for example, or turning more a certain way, and it just seems a real struggle. Or, your trainer says, 'Yes, that's it!!! Now hold it …' and you feel contorted, while the horse doesn't feel any different at all! It can be frustrating for both the rider and trainer (and obviously the horse) when, despite persistent reminders and consistent effort, rider corrections remain stubbornly beyond reach. Do any of the following seem familiar?

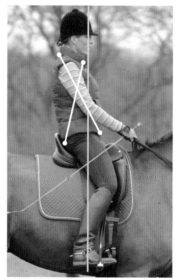

Above and right: Look at these photos – can you see how, if we were to draw a diagonal line from each of the rider's hips to her opposite armpit, the diagonals wouldn't look the same length? The cross point should be right in the centre, not shifted off to one side. If one diagonal appears clearly longer than the other one, or the 'cross point' isn't in the centre, the boxes are mis-stacked! The upper and lower photos to the far right show more correct positions.

I try hard with my position – my trainer tells me all the time to make this or that correction, but:

1. It's fine while I'm thinking about it and my horse definitely feels better, but a couple of minutes later I've forgotten and I've gone wrong again.

   (We'll discuss later how conscious corrections sometimes get lost in the mix of all the other things you have to think about whilst riding.)

2. It feels really awkward – sometimes even hurts – when I get into the position my trainer wants me to adopt.

3. I make the correction, but my horse stiffens against me.

This is where it is likely that your body is not functioning intrinsically biome-chanically as well as it could be, and your ability to absorb the horse's movement equally through both sides of your body is diminished. This affects your core, and your balance, and increases the risk of stress, strain and injury. If there are restrictions in how your body is working on the inside, making your position *look* better on the outside by following all the usual cues (poor ones: 'Sit up straight – heels *down!*' – or better ones: 'Lengthen your spine', or even my own phrase 'Headlights!!') can often be ineffectual. In the worst case, superimposing an outer layer of 'looking nice' on top of an inner layer which is struggling can be damaging as yet another compensatory mechanism is brought into play.

The solution? Take care of both form *and* function, or preferably, function and form in that order!

In the next chapter, I'll introduce you to a set of simple and straightforward exercises that yield quite remarkable results. If you practise them as prescribed, these exercises make a massive impact on the biomechanical function of your body. The order in which you proceed through the programme is of paramount importance. They will help to reduce low-grade muscle spasm, improve nerve mobility and joint range. This means that your body progressively assumes 'normal' function. You'll start to unwind old and new patterns of restriction and compensation – once you've spent a while concentrating on this aspect, we can then start to stabilise you with some core work.

Once function has been improved, we can seriously get down to business with the 'form' aspect. In reality though, form very often improves automatically as a result of better intrinsic biomechanics: once muscle balance and joint func-tion are addressed, riders find that they ride for longer periods without feeling that they need to make a positional correction; the misdemeanours occur less often, or the corrections only need to be a fraction of what they once were, since the misdemeanours are now much smaller. A related advance is that, because riders are really much more aware of how it feels when it is really good, the misdemean-ours are now consciously noticeable (which indicates the development of 'feel'), which leads to earlier self-correction . What we are left with then, is probably just postural habit. This can be worked on both on and off the horse and, seriously effectively, in the mind! See Chapter 11 to find out more about how to do this.

Your horse's posture and movement patterns

Of course, your horse has his own postural and alignment patterns, and how he arranges his body in movement will also influence you and encourage you to sit in particular ways. If he has tendencies to use one of his hind legs a bit more than the other (just like us being left- or right-handed) to push himself along, there will

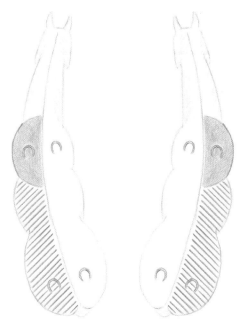

Above: Natural asymmetry in the horse means that his spine, in particular his neck, will adopt a slightly curved position, with a tendency to load one lateral pair of legs more than the other. You can see how, on the inside of the bend, the neck muscles tend to be stuck 'short' and are therefore harder to stretch. The shoulder muscles abduct that foreleg just a bit more during the stance phase than the one on the outside of the bend, causing the horse to fall out or 'leak' through the opposite shoulder. The neck muscles on the outside of the bend are 'stuck' long. The pink areas represent the areas that 'leak' energy. The hatched areas show the hind leg that offers the greater propulsive power.

also be a difference in how his pelvis rolls from side to side, how his spine and ribcage swing from left to right, which of his forelegs bears the brunt of this unequal pushing force, and which way his neck bends more easily. Given that every horse has these loading and movement patterns, you can see how important it is to ensure that everything which has an influence on the horse's movement really needs to function as helpfully as possible in order to minimise the risk of discomfort and possible injury. Remember, we have a responsibility to our horse to absorb his movement so that we don't block the thrust coming from his hindquarters through his spine. If we have a mechanical dysfunction which does restrict or block the flow, it certainly affects performance and causes him to compensate in his movement patterns – this can lead to training and behavioural problems, saddle fitting issues and even lameness.

In *Pilates for Riders* I explained that the 'neutral spine' we are aiming for is a *dynamic* neutral, a position that we can move out of when we need to apply aids and then return to when the aid is no longer required. Still photos can only capture a snapshot in this sequence. Look again at the photos on page 20. Can you tell whether the horse is influencing how the rider sits, or whether it is perhaps the rider influencing how the horse is going? No, neither can I, from a still picture. You will see that there are slight anomalies in practically every picture in this book which could be criticised for not being 'perfect' – even the ones which are intended to show good examples! This is because riding is, above all else, about movement, not stillness. When the body has to contend with multiple forces, it is possible that a picture-perfect position could be forced or braced, and yet not be functionally helpful for the way of going at that particular moment. Having tried the 'I must hold myself in this marvellous position at all costs' approach, I prefer not to do this, and (although of course I self-evaluate whilst riding and make corrections where necessary), I instead work seriously on asymmetries and imbalances with carefully chosen corrective exercises and awareness techniques so that better riding develops organically and progressively. That said, whilst I am only too aware of the areas in which my own riding has definite room for improvement, the road I have travelled to achieve my current level of equitation so far is a long and winding one!

Regarding the impression of horse and rider working together though, even when looking at a combination in real life, it can be hard to tell which is the driving 'balancing (or unbalancing!) force' unless you can do a thorough physical assessment of both separately and then together. This is, of course, unless there is an obvious factor such as a rider persistently making an error of balance, for example rising too high in the trot and coming down behind the movement every stride (as described in Chapter 6), or poor timing of application/cessation of aids which clearly affects the horse. It is also understandable that even a very experienced rider can be adversely affected by a loss of balance or sudden reactions of a young or nervous horse. It would be sensible therefore to work on the rider's balance and timing in the first example, and the horse's in the second. In many cases, however, it is irrelevant; whilst we can make major changes in balance, posture and function in both the horse and the rider separately, *once they are working together* the partnership needs to be treated as simply that: one unit. They are inextricably linked, and of course the balance of one is directly influencing the balance of the other, with all the combinations of compensatory patterns between the two which that involves.

In Chapter 9 we will be looking at some exercises to help you determine where and how your horse may find certain movements easier to the left or to the right, and how you can help him through simple techniques both on the ground and from the saddle; work to develop equal flexibility both ways, and strength. The resulting improved symmetry and balance make it easier for you to maintain a centred and balanced position on top of your horse, which in turn helps him to move with more grace and fluidity beneath you. This helps to create an upward spiral of useful and easily channelled energy rather than a downward spiral of confusion, mixed signals and frustration between the two of you. Have a look at the diagram on page 22 to see common examples of asymmetry; left- or right-footed horses.

Many factors including trauma, repetitive movement patterns (i.e. being ridden in a certain way with perhaps dubious aiding/positioning/loading on the rider's part), saddle fitting, foot balance and pathological/genetic issues do indeed complicate matters with regard to how a horse uses his body in terms of bending and rotating through the spine and loading the limbs, which is why it is imperative that any training programme includes a comprehensive and cohesive approach to health and well-being in order to maximise performance. Over time, a rider whose weight is consistently distributed too far forward, back, or to the left or right can affect the horse's movement and limb loading to such an extent that changes in the horse's gait patterns (and even lameness) can occur. The rider whose body is significantly restricted or ineffectual on one side also affects the flow of energy from the horse's hind legs, through the back and neck to the mouth. Again, over time, this blocking of energy, even on a subtle level, can result in a reduction of freedom in the horse's gait. Likewise, the horse with imbalances, asymmetries, lack of balance and coordination can also affect the rider's body in the same way.

The saddle

We need to be aware of the interface between the rider and horse – the saddle – and understand that just as the saddle needs to suit the *horse* perfectly with regard to the tree shape, the length (many saddle fitters do not take into account the precise length of the horse's ribcage – a saddle which is too long and pressing any further back than the eighteenth rib can cause all sorts of problems) and the width, it is crucial that the saddle is of a suitable width through the twist and seat for the *rider*. A saddle that is too wide for the horse will encourage the rider to roll the pelvis or tip forward as the pommel drops to low.

A saddle that is too narrow for the horse can encourage the opposite pattern of rolling onto the back of the seat bones and flattening the rider's lumbar curve as the cantle tips back. Even if correctly fitted for the horse though, certain types of saddle will encourage the rider's pelvis to be extremely upright, or even roll it forward. If this is excessive, the rider would benefit from choosing a saddle with a wider twist (though not so wide as to affect the fit to the horse). Other saddles encourage the rider's pelvis to roll backwards. This could be because of a twist which is unsuitably wide for the pelvis. From the rider's perspective, choosing twist width carefully with the advice of highly skilled and qualified saddle fitter can be a useful corrective strategy provided that the rider's body is

Right: The effect on the rider of a saddle being too wide for the horse.

Far right. The effect on the rider of a saddle being too narrow for the horse.

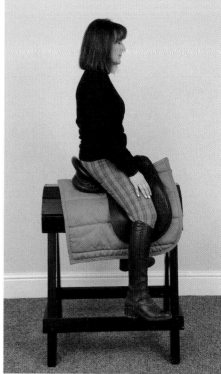

correctly prepared to adopt the new position. A saddle which is an inappropriate fit for the rider or horse can cause discomfort for both, but forcing a rider into 'neutral' when their body isn't used to it can also be uncomfortable. A correctly fitting saddle for horse and rider, plus the exercise programme detailed in the next few chapters, will help to develop a correct neutral position in the saddle which feels natural.)

There are excellent saddle fitters around who give the horse's shape and movement their full consideration, whilst also taking into account the rider's conformation and postural idiosyncrasies; the trick is finding them! When you have a new saddle fitted, or even your usual saddle checked, your saddle fitter should always watch you ride in walk, trot, canter and also any other movements which you are performing regularly in order to evaluate properly how you, your saddle and your horse are interacting together. It is particularly helpful to try to ensure that, when you schedule a saddle check, you also have your horse assessed and treated if necessary by a good physical therapist – and yourself, too!

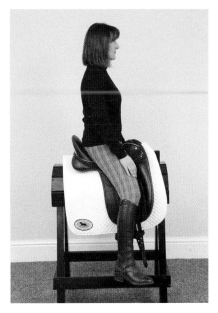

This saddle is helping the rider to sit effortlessly in a good, neutral alignment without tension.

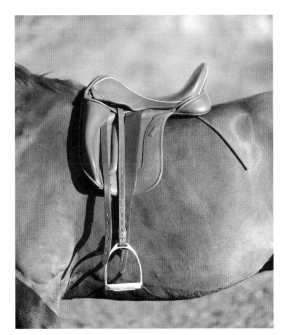

The orange line on the photo marks the horse's last rib – the saddle should not protrude further than this. Look how this one does: if this horse were ridden in a saddle this long (which he was, before I had him) it would put pressure on an unsupported area of his spine and potentially make him sore (which it did).

Having a very skilled saddle fitter who can offer a service to meet the needs of both you and your horse is essential.

The support team

Having yourself assessed and treated if necessary is another important piece of the jigsaw; there are some therapists who are qualified to treat both humans and horses, which is very helpful, especially if they are able to offer a functional or intrinsic biomechanical assessment of both you and your horse together. People ask me whether it is better to visit a physiotherapist, an osteopath, a chiropractor or some other type of manual therapist when they are in pain; this is a question which is impossible to answer in general terms – it all depends on the individual practitioner's skills and experience and your (and your horse's) needs. But if you are not in pain and require an Intrinsic Biomechanical Assessment to help your performance and prevent injury, then a Biomechanics Coach™ such as myself would help by seeing how your 'boxes are stacked up' and would be able to provide you with personalised corrective techniques. As regards therapists though, probably the best advice is to use one who has been recommended to you by someone whose opinion you really trust – your trainer perhaps, your vet, or a very knowledgeable friend. I have a network of therapists of different modalities who I always recommend to clients, and I have faith in their judgements. I do find it frustrating when, having recommended a particular person because of their special skills and experience, people instead use the local 'expert' simply because they are cheaper or other people on their yard are having group appointments. If someone has been strongly recommended to you it is usually for a good reason; their opinion is worth having and worth paying for!

CHAPTER TWO

Biomechanics of Balance

Understanding the core

In the previous chapter I mentioned that restrictions in pelvic function can affect the efficiency of your 'core', so I'll begin by explaining this further. The 'core' is definitely a buzzword in the equestrian world at the moment – we are inundated with recommendations for Pilates; top competitive riders at global events are showcasing their hard 'core' training regimes, and many classical trainers are encouraging of ways of developing more 'core stability'.

I started to explore the concept of 'the core' and core stability in my previous book *Pilates for Riders*, which also explores very effective breathing techniques in detail, explains how to engage your body to deliver a half-halt and give seat aids for downward transitions, and also offers an exercise plan for developing your core and other areas of your body with a selection of pure Pilates exercises, with modifications. Now let us delve a little more deeply into the biomechanics of how, as a rider, your body is required to work.

It's no secret that Pilates as an exercise form is a phenomenal complementary discipline to riding – it shares very similar goals and principles of awareness, control of mind and body, concentration and more. It can be used by skilled teachers for clinical and rehabilitation purposes with incredibly precise application, which can make an amazing difference within the body; it can be life-changing. However, it is also true that some people find Pilates, general core work or other techniques designed to improve alignment, flexibility and strength positively unhelpful. This is often because they are starting these core strength or conditioning programmes whilst there is dysfunction already present. Here, we are going to look at preparatory exercises designed to be used *before* starting core stability or strength training, which will help your body to become intrinsically biomechanically sound; this first phase ensures that your fundamental pelvic and spinal mechanics are 'normalised' and so provide the building blocks for normal movement. The exercises help to reduce any sub-clinical muscle spasm and target some nerve mobility issues. This phase is referred to as 'before the core', because typically people will start their early exercise programmes with core stability-type exercises when they are simply not ready. That is why normal Pilates helps some people but not others. Why would you want to stabilise your body in a biomechanically incorrect position? It is much more beneficial to 'normalise' how your body is working, then 'stabilise' yourself with core work, so that you are not training simply to compensate for your biomechanical problems, but instead developing correct movement patterns.

Awareness and improvement of your alignment and weight distribution (your extrinsic biomechanics, or 'form') assists your horse in developing his balance and carriage. Ensuring that your body is also intrinsically aligned allows the mechanisms within, which are responsible for maintaining symmetry, dynamic stability and efficient shock-absorption, to work correctly. Horses are so sensitive to changes in a rider's extrinsic and intrinsic biomechanics that working on both can revolutionise your riding. One aspect affects and can actually put the other into effect in any case. Your movement patterns shape your posture and vice versa, both on and off your horse. His movement patterns and posture influence yours too. Unwinding tension in the body and mind will open the door to core sense and fabulous, fluid, fully functional movement. Your performance potential is amazing!

The traditional 'core' has different definitions, depending on where you look. Often, in the Pilates sense, the particular muscles referred to are the transversus abdominus, the pelvic floor muscles ('floor' of the Pilates powerhouse) the diaphragm (the 'ceiling') and the multifidus. The obliques are also important. Some definitions refer to core muscles as 'postural'

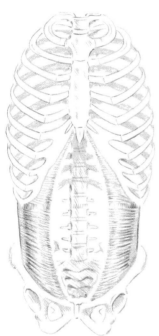

The core is often thought of as only the transversus abdominus.

muscles, the ones which support and attach directly to the spine, and this would, of course, describe very deep muscles within the body. However, such definitions broaden the range of muscles quite considerably. Let's take the view that core muscles support the spine; then surely any muscle which attaches to it and has a direct influence on how the spine is aligned, could be termed a core muscle.

Now it is getting interesting, because we're including the psoas, attaching onto the last thoracic vertebra, most of the lumbar vertebrae and the discs in between, and onto the inside/top of the femur. This muscle, along with the iliacus, can flex your hip; it can laterally rotate it; it can also be involved in flexing your spine sideways, and rotating it, and even extending it! It plays an important role in managing the front-to-back balance in your pelvis. We've also got the piriformis into play, which attaches to the front of your sacrum and to the top of your femur. This muscle has a complex relationship with the psoas, and, with it, can often be co-responsible for the body functioning in the opposite way on one side from the other, for example your pelvis being rotated forwards on one side and backwards on the other. The piriformis can rotate your extended hip outwards, but if your hip is flexed to between 70 and 90 degrees or more, it swaps function to rotate it inwards! It also acts powerfully to abduct your thigh (bring it outwards) away from your body and therefore is a major player in whether you can sit centrally in the saddle. If one thigh abducts more easily than the other, it becomes rather tricky to sit square. Then there's the quadratus lumborum (QL), attaching on your bottom rib, to your lumbar vertebrae and to the top of your iliac crest (back of your pelvis). We could also include the scalenes, which attach to your cervical vertebrae and the top of your ribcage. There are all the erector spinae as well as the very deep muscles of the spine, and many others too. We tend to think of these muscles more in terms of movement than posture, but in fact they have major influence on how you stand, sit, move and certainly ride.

We've then got to consider how the opposite partners of these muscles are working – when the psoas is working in its role as a hip flexor, then its opposite partner would be the gluteus maximus, extending the hip. In fact this has attachments on the sacrum and coccyx (the very bottom of the spine) so could also be considered a core muscle; it certainly has a huge influence on the integrity of pelvic function. The piriformis, in its role as an abductor, would be opposed by the adductors (which move the thigh inward) in your inner thighs. In its action as a lateral rotator, we'd be looking at the medial rotators; tensor fascia lata and gluteus medius and minimus. QL, as a lateral flexor of the spine, is opposed by itself, on the other side! However, if it is tight or restricted on both sides, because it is pulling on both sides simultaneously, the result is often a lumbar spine stuck in extension. In this case therefore, the muscles providing the opposite action would be the spinal flexors – the fibres more at the front of your body of the internal and external obliques, plus the rectus abdominus.

If any one of the 'opposite partner' muscles is compromised in its proper function, even if not directly attached to the spine, the alignment of the spine is affected because of the reciprocal relationship. In fact, if the tension of any one muscle anywhere in your body alters, over time this has influence on your posture; your whole body is one wonderful, complex mesh and we could say that, in fact, *any* muscle is a core muscle! However, we will address a number of the muscles just mentioned further in this book: intrinsic biomechanical inefficiencies within these in particular prevent good core control and the required balance and stability you need as a rider.

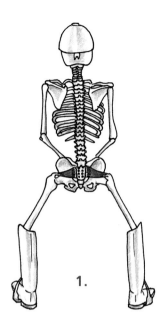

1.

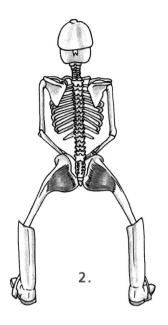

2.

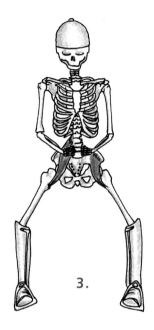

3.

1. Piriformis – hugely influential on your pelvic function and balance in the saddle.

2. The gluteus maximus: instrumental in front-to-back balance of your hips, along with the psoas, and can inhibit or release movement in the horse.

3. The psoas (left), with its many functions, has enormous power to restrict or release your horse's fluidity. The iliacus is shown on the right.

4. The gluteus medius rotates the hip inward, but as it also abducts the hip, is a major player in terms of whether you sit centrally in the saddle.

5. The quadratus lumborum is a lateral flexor and so influences whether you tip or slip to one side with the pelvis or ribcage.

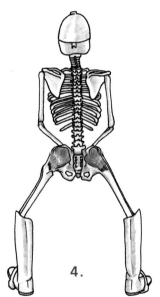

4.

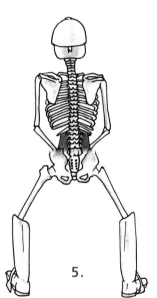

5.

Muscle spasm

If muscles around your pelvis and hip joint go into spasm as a protective mecha-nism (which is really very common – but see the note on page 32), it can wreak all sorts of havoc on your position, such as making your legs appear to be different lengths (owing to the iliac crest, which is the wing of the pelvis, rotating forwards and down or backwards and up, in relation to the sacrum or tailbone) and all sorts of far-reaching effects from compressing the facet joints on one side of your spine (this can be very uncomfortable) and causing a whole host of other muscles in your back, and even your shoulders, to also activate this protective mechanism of going into spasm. This has a marked effect on your ability to maintain a following, elastic contact.

Shoulder muscles in spasm could heavily influence the fact that your elbows stick out, or one sticks out, or one sits higher than the other (there could also be other reasons for this, which could cause the ribcage to be drawn closer to the pelvis on one side), or you struggle to soften the rein, or you can't stop giving it away! Once there is a 'dysfunction' present, our bodies compensate by trying to restore a balance to the structure, and dissipating it elsewhere (think ripples in a lake) so it tends to have impact around the body – pelvic dysfunction often affects shoulder function too, as indeed, the shoulder can affect the pelvis. Patterns of dysfunction or compensation can travel up and down, left to right or vice versa and especially through diagonal lines within the body. Remember the pictures in the previous chapter of the diagonal imbalances on the rider (page 20); we really need both diagonal connections to be fully operational. If we catch this process early, we can help to release muscle spasm before the body has to compensate for it.

Note that in using the term 'spasm' here, I don't mean the type of spasm which occurs when you suddenly feel intense pain – this requires treatment from a qualified physical therapist. Here I am referring to gradual muscle spasm that builds up in a muscle that is protecting a vulnerable joint/area. You won't necessarily feel or be aware of this at all. (In my case, I was convinced that all my problems were in my right side, as this was where I felt discomfort. In fact, the intrinsic biomechanical restrictions were mostly on the left! When these were resolved, my right side was no longer uncomfortable.)

Muscles that are stuck in this state of spasm, neither 'fully on' nor 'fully off', become dysfunctional because not only do they struggle to relax, they can't use their full power capacity either. They are switched on to an unnecessary degree, all the time, because the 'you can relax now' instruction from your brain has been lost somewhere along the way. The anti-spasm exercises in this chapter help the 'relax' message to get through properly again. But there's another problem with muscles being stuck, because in using a fair amount of needless energy, their muscle partners (the ones that create the opposite action) can become what is termed 'reciprocally inhibited', which means they aren't working properly either! So, first we are going to reduce potential spasm in the areas that are most commonly restricted in the riders I work with, then, when we have given the body a fair amount of time in which to do this (this is why it is *very* important to follow at least this section to the letter!) we can move on to waking up their muscle partners which have become sleepy, and then finally conditioning the main players themselves.

Example of muscle spasm – the piriformis ripple effect

Muscles work in groups and chains and are connected together by connective tissue called fascia, or myofascia. Think of a string of sausages – your muscles are the sausage meat and the fascia is the thin skin surrounding the meat, giving it structure and form. In fact, this tissue interweaves all your muscles – and bones, too – in a sort of web: a whole complex web of sausages! There are various lines of 'pull' in these chains of muscles (sometimes called 'slings' or 'tracks') running in a variety of directions through the body – up and down the front, back and sides of your body, and also around it in spirals, which means they cross your body diagonally. This in turn means that often, any dysfunction in a localised area is not isolated to one muscle, but is far-reaching as it continues throughout a chain because the tensions also become altered in other muscles that are connected to it. This is also why, when there is a functional restriction present, making a change to one area of your riding position can send another a bit out of whack – i.e., you straighten your seat and then your ribcage goes off to one side. Likewise, improving function in one area can also have benefits elsewhere in the body – for instance, improving mobility in the pelvis can have a positive effect on the shoulder, and even vice versa. Body workers, exercise professionals and movement therapists are becoming more and more aware of the 'fascial slings' in the body and how they influence free, easy movement and also stability in our bodies. Look at the diagram below to see common effects of the piriformis going into spasm: this happens as a protective mechanism for the pelvis, or more specifically the sacroiliac joint. You'll see a number of issues. Over time, this can cause niggling discomfort and even pain.

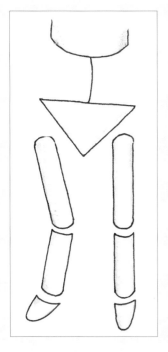

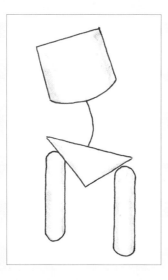

The piriformis in spasm could ripple upwards and result in muscles around the shoulder on the opposite side also going into spasm, as the tensions are altered through the connected muscles between. The ripple effect could also travel downwards, affecting leg function and altering knee and foot alignment.

Calibration exercises

Now though, we'll begin the calibration series – and this can be quite mind-blowing.

Incorporating the 'normalise' exercises and targeted conditioning work (Chapter 3) into my own riding and teaching has yielded quite remarkable results, and allowed me to discover better movement, balance and connection with my horse than I had thought possible. These exercises correlate directly with a specific screening programme that, as a qualified Biomechanics Coach™, I use with my clients. The screening process, which is repeated every time I see them, identifies restrictions within the body. Then a very prescriptive exercise plan is developed which targets specific areas; this changes accordingly to meet the intrinsic biomechanical needs of the client as their body adapts to improving function. The beauty of the anti-spasm exercises I have selected to present in this book is that if you need them, they'll work for you, but if your body doesn't happen to specifically require them, they'll have no adverse effect. (Note, though, that every rider I have so far assessed has required most, if not all of them!) The screening process and biomechanics coaching programme has been developed with a huge amount of research, evidence and experience by Intelligent Training Systems™ founder Martin Haines. Its cutting-edge application is now used worldwide to help élite athletes in every sport to maximise performance and minimise the risk of injury, and to facilitate improvement for any keen sportsperson serious about their dream, whether that is enjoying their hobby on a Sunday afternoon or aiming for competitive success. It also assists in enabling people who have been off work with back pain to return to work and live the full life they wish to lead. Note, however, that if you are currently in pain you must consult a medical professional before starting the programme. If you experience pain (not just 'newly worked muscle sensation') whilst, or after, doing any of the exercises in this book, stop and consult a medical professional or physiotherapist.

Calibration exercises for the pelvis

Below is the first set of anti-spasm exercises that concentrate on the pelvis. You will be using these in the first week of your ten-week programme, and you *must* start with these before continuing any further. Although we'll be concentrating on these vital components for only the first couple of weeks (I'm trusting you to follow the instructions for at least that amount of time to the letter!), anti-spasms can generally be maximally useful for up to six weeks from when you start the programme. After this time, stretches and then muscle conditioning are likely to be of greater benefit. In any case, though, it is advisable to do anti-spasms before you ride in order to maximise your joint mobility and get your core connections communicating. I would say that they are a useful tool to integrate into your pre-ride warm-up on a permanent basis, as it only takes a sudden spook, buck or jolt up the backside from an unexpected short stride before a jump to knock your suspension system (muscles around your hips and pelvis) slightly out of balance. However, the better your alignment and symmetry and the more conditioned you are (supple and strong), the less likely this is to happen.

These three exercises help to reduce and progressively eliminate any low-grade spasm in the muscles around your hip and bottom, which can be involved in functional leg length discrepancy and lack of mobility in your pelvis, restriction in shock-absorption capacity and also pelvic tilts, shifts and rotations.

▶ Leg press – anti-spasm for the glutes

Sit with your legs about hip-width apart. Lift your left knee up towards your chest and clasp your hands behind your thigh to support the weight. Using only 20% of your maximum possible effort (see box opposite), press your thigh downwards into your hands without allowing your hands to be moved. Hold this low-level isometric (static) contraction for 20 seconds.

Let the leg go and place your foot on the floor for a few seconds, then lift your leg again and press your thigh down into your hands again immediately for three more sets of 20 seconds. Remember, it is important to only use around 20% of your maximum possible muscular effort – using more will not make it work better!

Now repeat, this time pressing your right thigh into your hands.

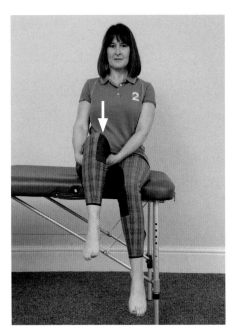

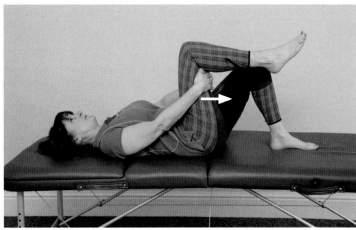

Left: Leg press (the arrow shows the intended direction of movement).

Above: You can also perform the leg press lying down – if you're struggling for time, you can do this in bed morning and night. That's twice a day done already!

TOP TIP

To find your '20%', first press as hard as you can to find your 100% effort level. Then only use about half this pressure; this will be your 50%. Then use just under half that, to find around 20%. It will probably feel just a little more than simply the weight of your leg.

This general process can be used to find your '20%' for all other exercises where that level of effort is required.

▶ 4 sign – anti-spasm for the hip rotators

Sit with your legs about hip-width apart. Cross your right ankle over your left thigh just above your knee. Using only 20% of your maximum possible effort, press your ankle into your thigh as if you were trying to move it to the right, but without actually doing so. If you are doing this correctly, you will be pivoting around your right hip and so your right knee should want to lift as you press your right ankle down against your immovable left thigh. So, to prevent this happening and to ensure it is a 'static' contraction where no movement takes place, put your hand on top of your right knee. Hold this isometric (static) contraction for 20 seconds.

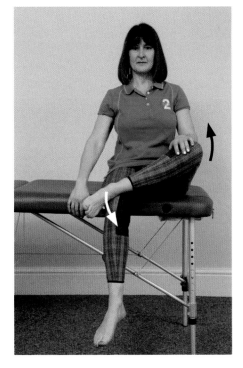

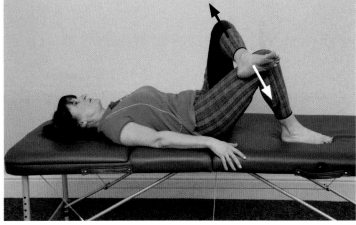

Left: 4 sign (the arrow shows the intended direction of movement).

Above: You can also perform the 4 sign lying down – another one you can do in bed!

Release the pressure, place your foot on the floor for a few seconds, return to the starting position and then immediately press again for three more sets of 20 seconds (four in total). Remember it is important to use only 20% of your maximum possible muscular effort.

Now repeat all four sets of 20 seconds each, this time crossing your left ankle over your right thigh.

If you find the 4 sign position really difficult to get into or seriously uncomfortable, do this version instead, pressing your knee outwards against your hand. It is very important that if you do this whilst sitting, you are only perched on the very edge of the seat so that your hip is not flexed much at all.

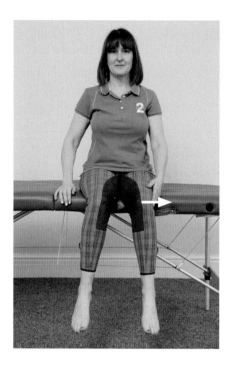

▶ Hip flexor – anti-spasm for (you guessed it) the hip flexors

The side-lying version shown in the photo opposite is best for this, but in fact it is probably more practicable for you to intersperse a standing one throughout the day, so I have detailed this one. Stand near any object that is stable enough to not move if you press your knee or thigh against it. Using only 20% of your maximum effort level, press your knee or thigh into the object as if you were trying to bring your knee up to your chest (but whatever you're pressing against is stopping it). Hold this isometric contraction for 20 seconds.

Release the pressure and then immediately press again for three more sets of 20 seconds (four sets in total). Remember to use only about 20% of your maximum possible muscular effort.

Have a look at what sort of difference can be made after just one application of these hip flexor anti-spasm exercises: the photos, opposite below, show genuine before and after shots.

Note

The exercise programme herein is specifically designed to fit in with busy lives and deliver short, but very effective, workouts of around 10 minutes each. However, stages incorporating anti-spasms are slightly different from the following ones as, in order to work most effectively, they require you to split that time up into small chunks throughout your day. Anti-spasms need to be performed *four times a day*, and especially before and preferably after any activity which would be likely to revert your body into unhelpful patterns, for example riding, mucking out a few stables or sitting in a car for a long time. They only take a little time to do, but are so very worth the effort. As soon as you are through this phase, your workout time will condense and you'll only have to do your exercises once a day.

Left: Hip flexor anti-spasm whilst standing (the arrow shows the intended direction of movement).

Above: Another lying down version to try – do this version perhaps morning and night. Press your knee against the resistance of your top leg.

Below left: This is the position I use to assess hip flexor range. (You don't need to do this; it is just to illustrate how effective the exercise is). This is Sally, before doing the anti-spasm exercise. *Below right:* Look at the difference 3 minutes afterwards! Imagine how much more she'll be able to follow her horse's movement through her hips.

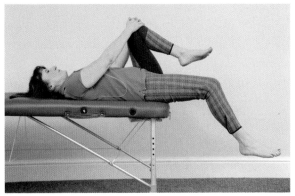

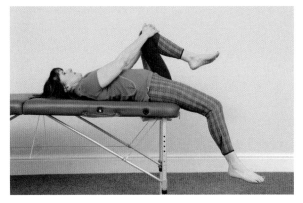

CHAPTER THREE

Rider Conditioning for Balance and Symmetry

We all know that life with horses can be hectic and, after a long day, doing something physical for your own body can sometimes seem low on your priority list. However, remember that your body and its shock-absorption capacity has major influence on your horse's health and performance. In this chapter we will discover how 10 minutes, which is around what the mini-workout programmes are designed to take, can make a world of difference. Remember, they all target better biomechanical efficiency very specifically for you as a rider.

If you seriously want to make a significant difference to your riding, do one of these short, sharp and effective programmes every day once you're past week 2. If you happen to have extra time, or are particularly motivated, double up and pick two sessions. If you have a particular event coming up, maybe a competition which is important to you, or some other significant time with your horse when you want to be in peak condition, try doubling up and doing two workouts every day for a few days beforehand – this could be one after the other, or maybe one first thing in the morning and one later on in the day. I particularly selected the exercises here to make them as easy as possible to fit in and to really deliver results. Follow this ten-week programme to revolutionise your riding!

Equipment, terminology and aims

The first few weeks require no equipment at all, but to gain maximal benefit from your programme in the shortest time I have included exercises which do make use or small items of equipment, which you will be able to purchase inexpensively – or for which you can easily find substitutes. From week 4 onwards, for example, we use spiky balls – but you can use two tennis balls instead. If you do wish to use spiky balls, shop or do an internet search for 'spiky massage balls'. You can get firm or soft ones of different sizes – we use firm ones of around 7–9cm for shoulders and piriformis release, but slightly larger soft ones for the hip flexor release. In the associated photos, as a progression for the core stablisers, we also show an exercise on a foam roller. This is a 15cm diameter full round foam roller of around 90cm long. You can get one (the cheaper ones, which are absolutely fine for home use, are usually white) using an internet search as sports shops don't usually sell them, or you can substitute a large, firm rolled-up towel. Simply lying on a foam roller for a few minutes without doing anything at all, apart from relaxing, is actually wonderfully effective for opening up the spine and chest and releasing tension – my clients all love them. If you do get one, practise just lying along it for a few minutes a few times before you use it for exercising, so you learn to balance without tension. You'll need to slide off it slowly after a few minutes and then just lie on the floor in the same position for a short while (knees bent, feet flat on the floor). It is an amazing feeling!

From week 5 onwards we use an 'isotoner'. To be honest, you can't really find a substitute for this, but it is such a useful piece of equipment I'm sure you won't mind getting hold of one. They are sometimes called 'Pilates rings' or 'magic circles' and are often sold now in supermarkets that sell fitness equipment, as well in as high street sports shops. You could also search the internet for them as they are readily available – you only need the cheapest version, not the more costly ones which are designed for heavy use in gyms and professional studios. You'll also need a Swiss/stability ball from week 5 onwards. Usually people need a 65cm ball, though if you are under 5ft 4in you may prefer a 55cm ball, or if you are 5ft 8in and above you'll need a 75cm ball.

In week 5, we start to engage the core. We've already discussed how we could interpret 'the core', but in terms of these exercises, it means a co-contraction of not only the transversus abdominus (the muscle that activates when you draw your tummy button towards your spine – this is termed 'hollowing') but other muscles too, around the front, sides and back of your body. We will call this co-contraction 'firing the core' or 'core fire'. Modern research shows that using all of these muscles, not just a hollowing action of the transversus abdominus, provides optimal spinal support and stability. For riders, 'core fire' is more beneficial than just hollowing. Try the following visualisation to help you feel this:

Imagine you are having a party. You need some balloons for your party, and a bag of them is ready next to you. I want you to pick an imaginary balloon from the bag (really reach your hand into the bag and pick one!) and notice what colour it is, and whether it is a round one or a long one. Stretch it out a few times to mobilise it – you know how tricky it can be to blow up some balloons! Bring it up to your lips and take a big breath – now start to blow into your balloon – the balloon doesn't want to expand though and seems hard to inflate – you'll have to blow a bit harder – really push the air through your lips. You can't blow any faster though, as the balloon just won't comply. Can you feel that all the muscles around the front, sides and back of your trunk have 'switched on'? That feeling is the one we're looking for; the core stabilisers firing.

From week 9 onwards we use a stretch band: if you haven't got one you can substitute a pair of old tights (thick ones!) or an elastic tail bandage.

We use the cue 'lengthen your spine' in Pilates all the time. I've even heard riding instructors use it too! In the following exercises, there are cues to lengthen your spine. This means creating space within the spinal column, to relieve the effects of compression. You can do this by imagining that there is a thread running right through your spine from the top to the bottom. If you were to gently pull on the end coming through the crown of your head, and at the same time gently pull on the thread coming down from your tailbone, your spine would elongate like a concertina opening. Try to practise this feeling of effortless elongation in your daily life. The exercise programme detailed below will help this to become a way of life, even when you aren't consciously thinking about it.

The programme

WEEK 1 Calibrating the hips

Three pelvic anti-spasms: leg press, 4 sign and hip flexor as detailed in Chapter 2. These should be performed every day, four times a day this week for maximum benefit.

WEEK 2 Calibrating the nerves

Every other day, perform the three pelvic anti-spasms as in week 1.
On the alternate days, perform the following series:

▶ QL wall glides (twice a day)

This exercise helps to reduce and progressively eliminate low-grade spasm in your quadratus lumborum muscles by mobilising the spine.

Stand sideways next to a wall or doorframe with your feet about 4in away from it, and together. Keep your elbow bent and keep the whole of your upper arm in contact with the wall throughout the exercise. Slowly slide your hips across to touch the wall, and then release away again. Repeat this small slide/gliding motion for a total of eight times.

Now turn around and repeat the eight glides on the other side. When you have completed these, do another set of eight on each side.

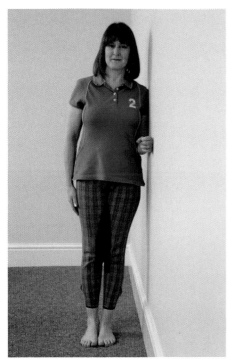 

Far left: Wall glides; start position.

Left: Touch the wall with your hips, then release.

▶ Slump (twice a day)

Sit with your legs dangling freely. Place your arms behind your back and curl your head and shoulders down a little bit so you're in a 'slump'. Flex the toes of your left foot upwards, and then slowly start to straighten your knee until you feel a slight stretch. Slowly return your lower leg (toes still flexed up) to release the stretch and go back to the start position, then repeat another seven times (eight in total). Do the same on the right leg, and then repeat another set of eight on the left leg and again on the right leg (each leg will have done sixteen movements in total).

Right: 'Slump'; start position.

Far right: Straighten your knee only to the point at where you feel a slight stretch.

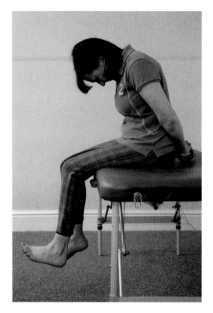

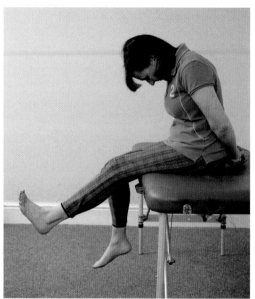

This exercise works as a nerve mobiliser – you might ask why this is important.

The sciatic nerve can become stiff or restricted in its mobility as it passes down the leg, branching out in various places This stiffness or restriction can be influenced by spasm or muscle tightness anywhere along its route – the piriformis in particular is often a sticking point if it is in spasm. The reason I am including the sciatic nerve here (a personal biomechanics programme includes assessing and improving mobility of other nerves too) is because of its influence in terms of giving leg aids and mobilising it can improve pelvic function too.

As riders, we need to have responsive and powerful hamstring (and calf) muscles in order to apply and release leg aids quickly and also to keep the lower leg in a correct and well-balanced position. Poor leg position can be a result of poor positioning of the pelvic and ribcage boxes, but it can also be rooted in the leg muscles themselves. If the hamstrings aren't working as well as they might, your lower leg might persistently stick forwards (usually coupled with over-working quadriceps muscles at the front of your thighs). If they require releasing or lengthening, the lower leg will often stay too far back (again, often the quadriceps here will also need conditioning for strength). Nerves don't particularly like moving fast, or stretching; muscles around the nerve will try to prevent this and can go into spasm as a protective mechanism. We don't tend to make high-velocity forward kicks as riders, but a similar action might happen as your bottom moves back and up away from the lower leg over a fence if the horse jumped in a way that took

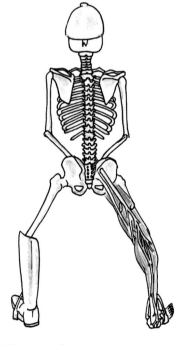

The route of the sciatic nerve.

you by surprise. This means that, when you feel that you are restricted at the back of your legs in certain movements (and most riders feel that their hamstrings are tight!), like sitting down in a neutral spine with your legs outstretched, or maybe on a 'roll down' exercise, it is very possible that it is actually the nerve that needs mobilising and the issue is not just hamstring tightness. Mobilising the nerve is a useful step in enabling the hamstrings, and other muscles along the route, to work efficiently, so they can be used and released when necessary. Practising the 'slump' improves hamstring mobility and range.

WEEK 3 Spinalign

Continue to do the pelvic and hip anti-spasms four times a day every other day and also before you ride. On alternate days, once a day, do the QL and slump, plus the following spinalign series to increase flexibility and mobility in the spine.

▶ Flexion – roll down against wall

This is a great flexion exercise for the spine as it helps to open up the spaces in between each vertebra and also with 'articulation'; this means you being able to move one bone at a time so each joint in the spine has mobility. When your spine articulates well you avoid chunks of vertebrae all moving together, which can cause hinge points and put excessive stress on particular areas of the spine.

- Start position: stand with your back against a wall with your feet about 1ft away so you have flexion in your knees. Spread the weight as evenly as possible between your two feet.

- Lengthen your spine.

- Curl your chin to your chest; feel the weight of your head and allow that weight to help you roll your spine down, bone by bone, away from the wall to create a 'C' shape in your spine. Make sure the back of your pelvis stays pressed to the wall and your tailbone feels heavy, as though it is being pulled down towards the floor.

- Let your arms hang very loosely and softly like a rag doll.

- When you have rolled as far as you can *without your knees bending or your pelvis coming away from the wall*, breathe in then, as you breathe out, begin re-stacking your spine from the bottom bone by bone. Visualise your tailbone drawing heavily down to the floor behind you to help you re-stack the lumbar vertebrae correctly, and draw in your lower abdominals to help you press each bone back onto the wall one by one.

- When you have re-stacked all the vertebrae (your head is the last thing to come up), lengthen your spine and drawn your shoulder blades gently back and down against the wall.

- Repeat three times, for a total of four.

ABOVE

Left: Flexion; start position.

Centre: Rolling down bone by bone.

Right: Only go to the point you can reach just before you need to increase the bend in your legs.

▶ Intensive side stretch

This exercise mobilises your spine in lateral flexion and lengthens the spine by stretching the chains of muscles at the sides of your body. When one is 'stuck' shorter than the other, it can give the impression of a 'collapsed hip' or dropped shoulder. If you spend a little longer stretching the tight side – you can take an extra two or three breaths within the stretch, or you could do two stretches on your tight side to every one on the easier side – it will help to stop you scrunching up whilst riding.

- Start position: stand about 1ft away from a doorframe or anything stable you can hang on to.

- Lengthen your spine.

- Cross your right leg over your left leg and hold the frame with your right hand.

- Inhale then, as you exhale, float your left arm out to the side, up and over to hold the doorframe; your body should make a 'C' shape.

- Breathe in then, as you breathe out, allow your body to really hang off the doorframe so the 'C' shape deepens. You should feel a really intensive stretch through the whole of your left side; thigh, hip, waist, ribs and arm. You can bend your right knee more to open further into the stretch.

- Breathing is a key to enhancing this stretch. Exhale as much as you possibly can – every last puff of air; even when you think your lungs are empty, there will be a little bit more you can squeeze out. Your in-breath will then be especially full, and the extra opening of the ribs as you inhale is very effective. Try to build up to staying in the stretch for around 45 seconds.

- Repeat on the other side, this time with your left leg crossed over your right.

- Repeat once more on each side.

BELOW

Left: Intensive side stretch; start position.

Centre: Float your arm up and over.

Right: Allow your body to 'hang' into the stretch.

▶ Intensive twist

This exercise increases your spine's rotational flexibility. It is useful for stretching and engaging the oblique muscles (side/waist muscles) and the particular chains of other muscles in your body which may contribute to unwanted twists, or lack of rotation capacity in your body. The chest opener, head and hip rolls, sundial and spine twist exercises in *Pilates for Riders* are also useful for this.

- Start position: sit on the floor with your legs extended.

- Lengthen your spine.

- Cross your right leg over your left with your foot flat on the floor.

- Rotate to the right, placing your left arm against your right thigh to gently pull your knee to the left. You should feel the stretch in your outer thigh.

- Breathe in and, as you breathe out, twist your body even more to reach behind you with your right hand.

- Keep your shoulders soft and your chest open and wide.

- Concentrate on your breathing within the twist – you may find that you are able to turn just a little bit further with each out-breath. Try to spend 30–45 seconds in the twist.

- Repeat, this time crossing your left leg over your right and twisting to the left. How does this feel? Can you still feel both seat bones on the mat? If you feel a difference between the two sides, hold the twist for a little longer on the more difficult side, or try two twists exercises on this side to every one on the easier side.

- Repeat once more each side.

Below left: Intensive twist; start position.

Below right: Into the twist.

▶ Crescent moon

This exercise mobilises your spine in extension and helps to lengthen chains of muscles at the front of your body, whilst engaging those at the back. If you spend much of the day sitting, either at a computer or maybe driving, the muscles at the front of your body can be stuck short, pulling you into a 'C' shape and leaving your back muscles longer and weaker in relation. It is important to remember, when thinking of 'core stability', that the back, as well as the front and sides of your trunk all need to work as a team.

- Start position; stand with your feet no wider than hip distance apart (although they can be together).

- Float both of your arms up to the ceiling and place your palms together.

- Look up at your hands and reach upwards as far as you can to make the front of your body, from your toes to your nose, as long as possible.

- With each in-breath, feel yourself opening up more and more – reach right through the tips of your fingers to the ceiling.

- Spend around 5–10 seconds in the stretch, but repeat for a total of four.

- Do two more roll-downs against the wall just to finish off.

Far left: Crescent moon; start position.

Left: Extending the spine.

WEEK 4 Shoulder calibrating (on alternate days)

On alternate days do the 'shoulder calibrating' series as detailed below; on the other days do *either* spiky (tennis) ball releases (see Chapter 5) or the flexicore series of exercises in Chapter 4. Ensure you've done both options during the week.

▶ Pectoralis minor anti-spasm

It is really difficult to get your shoulders back and down when the pectoralis minor muscle is in spasm or restricted. Releasing it will help you to open your chest much more easily.

You can do this exercise sitting or lying. Have a feel along your collarbone towards your shoulder. At the front of your shoulder you should feel a big knobbly lump. Press your fingers into this lump and then press your shoulder forward with only 20% of your maximum effort level into the resistance of your fingers. Hold this isometric (static) contraction for 20 seconds. Release and relax both arms for a few seconds, then come back to the start position and immediately push it forward for a further three sets of 20 seconds (four sets in total). Remember to use only 20% of your maximum effort level. Repeat all four sets on the other side.

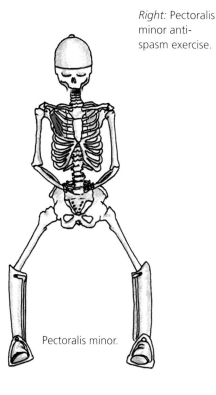

Pectoralis minor.

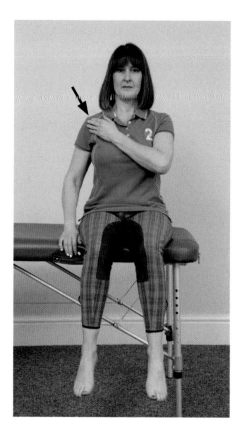

Right: Pectoralis minor anti-spasm exercise.

▶ Subscapularis anti-spasm

The subscapularis is a medial rotator and adductor of your humerus and is part of your 'rotator cuff' team of muscles. If any of the muscles which make up your rotator cuff aren't functioning properly, it disturbs the dynamics of the team and leaves the shoulder vulnerable to potential injury. It also affects how well you can keep your shoulder aligned, and therefore affects your contact when you ride.

Cup one fist with the other hand. Press both hands into one another with only 20% of your maximum effort level for 20 seconds. Relax both arms for a few seconds, then return to the start position and immediately press again to hold this isometric (static) contraction for three more sets for 20 seconds (four in total). Remember to use only 20% of your maximum effort level.

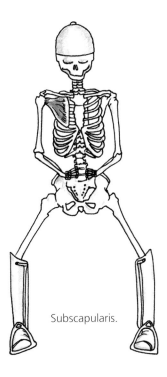

Subscapularis.

Subscapularis anti-spasm exercise.

Alternative: if you happen to be sitting in a chair with arms, you can put your own arms on the outside of the chair arms with your elbows bent. Press the palms of your hands inwards against the chair arms for your four sets of 20 seconds.

▶ Infraspinatus anti-spasm

The infraspinatus is a lateral rotator (so if it is working properly it should prevent 'chicken wing' elbow syndrome as you ride!) and adductor of the humerus. It is also part of the rotator cuff group and, like the subscapularis, if it isn't working as it should be it leaves the shoulder itself functionally compromised and vulnerable. How the infraspinatus is working (or not) will influence how well you can maintain a soft and consistent rein contact.

Make a 'Cossack' position with your arms, but make sure that the fingers of *both* hands are pressed against the *underneath* of your elbows. With only 20% of your maximum effort level, press the fingers and backs of your hands upwards against your elbows, as if you wanted to move your hands up and then out to the side. Hold this isometric (static) contraction for 20 seconds, then release and relax both your arms for a few seconds. Return to the start position and repeat for another three sets of 20 seconds (four in total). Remember to use only 20% of your maximum effort level.

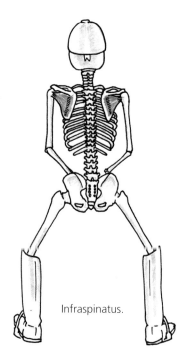

Infraspinatus.

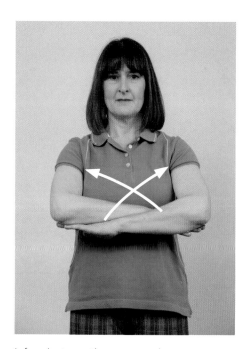

Infraspinatus anti-spasm exercise.

Alternative: if you prefer you can sit in a chair with arms and place your own arms on the inside of the chair arms with your elbows bent. Press the backs of your hands outwards against the chair arms for your four sets of 20 seconds.

▶ Upper trapezius anti-spasm

The upper trapezius muscles are often problematic if you struggle to keep your shoulders down and back. Releasing spasm here and then progressively conditioning the muscles will ensure that you no longer struggle with putting those lorry ramps up, or throwing rugs onto big horses!

Take your head over to the right. Place the fingers of your right hand just above your left ear. Using only 20% of your maximum effort level, press your head against the resistance of your hand as if you were trying to bring your head back to the middle. Hold for 20 seconds, then relax and come out of the position for a few seconds. Go back into the start position and immediately press your head against your hand in this isometric (static) contraction for a further three sets of 20 seconds (four in total). Remember to use only 20% of your maximum effort level.

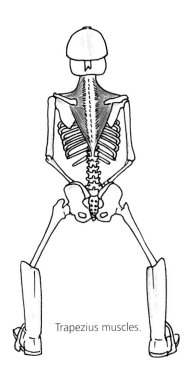

Trapezius muscles.

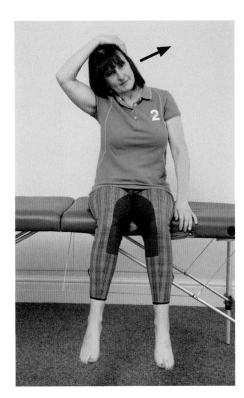

Upper trapezius anti-spasm exercise.

WEEK 5 Conditioning for balance (hip series 1)

Do hip series 1 as detailed below once a day every other day. On alternate days, do one of the following options: shoulder calibrating anti-spasms (four times a day), *or* spinal and nerve mobility (once a day), *or* Swiss ball programme (once a day – see Chapter 6). Ensure you have done all three options during the week.

To warm up
Bounce on your Swiss ball with 'swimming arms' as detailed in Chapter 6 for 1 minute.

▶ Glute/piriformis stretches

Lie on your back with your knees bent. Cross your right ankle over your left knee. Pull your left thigh towards you and press your left knee away. Hold for about 45 seconds, then repeat with the other leg.

Lie on your back with your knees bent. Cross your right thigh over your left thigh. Take hold of both of your ankles and draw them towards you; hold for about 45 seconds. Repeat with left thigh crossed over right thigh.

▶ Core-firing

Lie on your back with your knees bent. Lengthen your spine. Draw your navel towards your spine a little (so it is level with or just lower than your two hip-bones). Then, really firm up your waist muscles so that they feel hard to the touch – you can give them a pinch or a firm poke, or even wiggle your fingers into them and see if you can feel them wake up! You might have to press quite deeply. If you cough or laugh while your fingers are pinching your waist, you should feel them. Remember the balloon visualisation. During all the exercises from now on, you will need to activate your muscles at the front, sides and back of your trunk in this way in order to support your spine in position.

Practise holding your muscles active for 10 seconds. It is important to breathe too! Although this might seem tricky at first, keep practising and it will become easier. You might have to use slightly less effort to recruit your muscles until you can keep the breath flowing more easily, then increase it. Repeat this 10-second core-fire for another seven lots (eight in total). When you can feel your mid-section firm up consistently and easily every time you fire your core, you can practise using the same muscles on your horse at those times when you could do with being very stable – for instance, in downward transitions, or when you are changing the rein and there is potential for either you or your horse to lose some balance. This seat cue sequence is described in more depth in *Pilates for Riders*.

You can feel the muscles 'fire'.

Now try challenging the stability of your core-fire with some movement. We'll start simply, but further on in the programme there are more difficult options.

Float (imagine your leg is weightless!) your right leg up to 'tabletop' position (as if your calf was resting on a small coffee table) as you exhale. When you next exhale, float it back down again. Repeat this for a total of eight floats of each leg, aiming to keep your core fully fired throughout and no movement in your trunk *at all* – not even tiny rolls to the left or right, forward or back of your pelvis.

Leg float.

▶ Adductor and medial rotator conditioning

Whilst lying on your back with your knees bent, bring your feet as wide apart as you comfortably can and place your isotoner in between your thighs, just above your knees. Slowly and firmly squeeze the isotoner in between your thighs and release a total of eight times. Notice whether one leg appears to be able to squeeze in more than the other.

Now, keep your right leg completely still and just squeeze in for a total of eight times with your left leg – you'll feel that your thigh actually swivels inwards as well as moving inwards (this is working your medial rotators). Repeat the eight squeezes with your right leg now, keeping your left leg totally still.

With both legs now, as you did in the first place, squeeze inwards for a total of eight.

Left: Adductor and medial rotator conditioning; start position.

Right: Squeezing inwards with both legs.

WEEK 6 Conditioning for symmetry (hip series 2)

Hip series 2 as detailed below every other day (once a day). On alternate days *either* flexicore exercises as in Chapter 4 or spiky ball releases once a day – ensure you have done both options during the week.

To warm up
Bounce and 'swim' on a Swiss ball as detailed in Chapter 6 for 1 minute.
Perform glute/piriformis stretches as in week 5.

▶ Clam

Lie on your side with your knees bent and your underneath arm straight, palm facing up. Lengthen your spine and fire your core. Without your trunk and particularly your pelvis moving *at all*, open your top knee towards the ceiling, keeping your feet touching. Slowly lower, then repeat for a total of eight times.

Lie on your other side and repeat eight times. There are more difficult options for this exercise to be performed when you are comfortable with this one.

Clam; start position.

Open your top knee towards the ceiling.

▶ Side-lying balance – leg abduction

Lie on your side with your legs straight but a little forward of the rest of your body. Have your underneath arm outstretched, palm up, and your top arm supporting you on the floor in front of your chest. Lengthen your spine. Keeping your core firmly fired so there is absolutely no movement in your trunk at all, lift your top leg up to hip height or just above, then slowly return. Repeat for a total of eight, then perform eight on the other side. If you are confident with this exercise, you can try it with your arm along your thigh, which increases the balance challenge.

Right: Side-lying balance – correct alignment.

Above: Lift the top leg to hip height or just above.

▶ Abductor conditioning

Lie on your back with your knees bent. Place your legs through the isotoner and position it around your knees, or just above them. Lengthen your spine and fire your core. Slowly and firmly pull your legs apart against the resistance of the isotoner and release. Repeat a further seven times (eight in total). Notice whether one leg seems to be able to pull outwards better than the other.

Right: Abductor conditioning; start position.

Far right: Pull the isotoner apart with your thighs.

▶ Triple tap

Start on all fours, knees underneath hips and hands underneath shoulders. Lengthen your spine and fire your core. Keeping your trunk totally still, lengthen your left leg out behind you. Now open it wide to give the floor a gentle tap with your toes, move it back behind you and tap the floor gently, then sweep it across your right leg to tap the floor. Return to the start position and repeat the whole sequence again for a total of eight. See photos opposite.

Repeat with your right leg for a total of eight.

▶ Quad/hip flexor stretch

Kneel by a wall and place your left foot up on the wall. Slowly step onto your right foot and start to sit up – be careful, it can be tricky to balance! Lengthen your spine to keep your tailbone heavy, and squeeze your left bottom cheek to extend

Triple tap; start position.

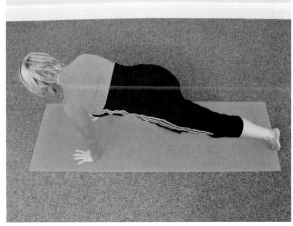

Lengthen your leg out behind you.

Tap it out.

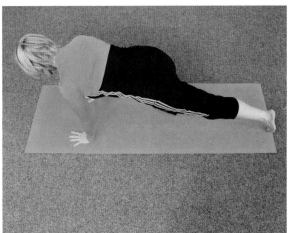

Tap it back.

Tap it across.

your hip a little bit and increase the stretch. Go steady with this one as it can be intensive – you'll be able to get closer to the wall and more upright in time.

Finally, repeat the glute/piriformis stretches as in week 5.

Quad stretch.

WEEK 7 Conditioning for better balance

Hip series 1, once a day every other day; on alternate days, spinal mobility or Swiss ball series (see Chapter 6) once a day – ensure you have done both options during the week

WEEK 8 Conditioning for contact

Perform the shoulder conditioning series as follows once a day every other day; on alternate days, do the flexicore series in Chapter 4, or spiky ball releases or hip series 2 once a day.

To condition for contact, we are now going to strengthen, amongst others, the shoulder muscles we have 'anti-spasmed'.

To warm up
Bounce on your Swiss ball with 'swimming arms' as detailed in Chapter 6 for 1 minute.

▶ Isotoner arm pull

You can do this sitting or standing.

Place your hands and wrists through the isotoner and position it in front of your body. Have your elbows slightly bent. Use your forearms, pull the isotoner apart as much as you can (keep your shoulder tops down) and then release. Repeat for a total of eight times.

Far left: Isotoner arm pull; start position.

Left: Engaging the lateral rotators to pull the isotoner apart.

▶ Istoner arm squeeze

You can do this sitting or standing.

Place the palms of your hands on the isotoner handles with your fingers straight (not curled around). Keep your elbows fairly close to your waist and squeeze the isotoner as if trying to touch the fingertips of each hand together. Release and repeat for a total of eight times.

Isotoner arm squeeze; start position.

▶ Isotoner waist squeeze

You can do this sitting or standing.

Place the isotoner between your waist and your upper arm, just above the elbow. Squeeze the isotoner towards your waist but at the same time turn your forearm outwards so your palm faces upwards rather than inwards. Release back to the start position then repeat for a total of eight times.

Repeat eight times on the other side.

Right: Isotoner waist squeeze; start position.

Far right: Squeezing inwards towards the waist.

▶ Lower traps

Lie on your tummy with a foam roller (or broom handle) underneath your finger-tips. Bring your forehead a tiny bit off the floor. Using only your shoulders and keeping your arms perfectly straight (your spine shouldn't change in alignment at all), draw your shoulder blades towards your bottom to roll the roller/broom handle towards you. It will only move a little bit. Then release and roll the roller/broom handle away from you again. Repeat this for a total of eight times, really focusing on the area below your shoulder blades, and feeling the muscles activate as you draw the roller towards you. See photos opposite, above.

▶ Upper traps

(Include within the 'conditioning for contact' series from week 10 onwards only).

Position your isotoner above your head as if you were wearing a halo. Lengthen your spine. Push the isotoner upwards and at the same time squeeze it a little bit. Release and lower it a little to return to your 'halo' position. Repeat for a total of eight times. See photos opposite.

Lower traps; start position.

It is only a small movement, but a useful one!

Upper traps starting 'halo' position.

Push your 'halo' upwards and squeeze.

WEEK 9 Conditioning for collection (hip series 3)

Perform hip series 3 as detailed below every other day once a day; on alternate days, spinal mobility *or* hip series 1 *or* Swiss ball series (see Chapter 6) once a day. Ensure you have covered different options during the week.

To warm up
Bounce on the Swiss ball with 'swimming arms' as detailed in Chapter 6 for 1 minute.

▶ Shoulder bridge

Lie on your back with your knees bent and your feet and knees about hip-width apart. Using your abdominals, tilt your pelvis backwards so that your lower spine is flattened to the floor. Then start to squeeze your bottom to peel your spine, bone by bone, off the mat. When your hips reach a point where your body makes a 'ski slope' position, all nicely in line, return your spine, bone by bone, to the mat. *Alternate* these with the upper body curls (below) Repeat for a total of eight each.

Shoulder bridge; start position.

The shoulder bridge 'ski slope'.

▶ Upper body curl

Float your arms up towards the ceiling. Use your upper abdominals to curl your head and neck up (take care to keep enough space to cradle a peach between your chin and collarbone); hold for a couple of seconds, then return. If you can, exhale to curl up, inhale to hold the position, then exhale to return your head and neck to the mat, before floating your arms back down. Don't worry though, if this is tricky – just keep breathing! Repeat alternately with the shoulder bridge exercise above for a total of eight times.

Upper body curl; start position.

Curling up.

▶ Glutes, standing with band

Stand facing something which is sturdy enough that you can tie your stretch band around it without it moving. Dining table legs are often useful, as are stair banisters! Loop the band around your right leg and hold on to whatever it is that the band is tied around. Lengthen your spine and really concentrate on keeping your core fired as you move – the spine should stay very still. Bring your right leg back by really using your right bottom muscles, then return to the start position. Repeat for a total of eight times. Be careful that you don't tip forwards or hollow your back – keep your tailbone heavy (a feeling of your 'water tipping out the back of the bowl' a little.

Right: Glutes, standing; start position.

Far right: Working the glutes.

Right and far right: Watch out for leaning forward or hollowing the back.

▶ Hip extension, prone with isotoner

This is more demanding than the standing exercise, so you might want to wait until after week 10 to try this.

Lie on your tummy with the istoner placed between your ankles and with your knees bent. Rest your forehead on your hands. If you feel pressure or discomfort in your lower back when you do this, place a cushion under your tummy. If the pressure or discomfort persists, do not do this exercise.

Keeping your core well fired, lift the isotoner up an inch or so. This is a small movement but requires some force to create! Lower back to your start position. Repeat for a total of eight times.

Glutes, prone; start position.

A small but challenging movement.

▶ Double hamstrings with band

Again, you'll need to be able to tie your band round something sturdy for this. Lie on your tummy and place the band around the back of both ankles. Rest your head on your hands. Pull the band as far as you can up towards your bottom, then release it back to the start position. Try to keep your trunk as stable as possible. Repeat for a total of eight times.

Double hamstrings, start.

Pull both ankles towards your bottom.

▶ Single hamstrings with band

In the same position as the first hamstrings with band exercise, place the band around just one ankle. Pull this ankle up towards your bottom as far as you can, then release back to the start position. Repeat for a total of eight times. Now repeat another set of eight, this time with the band around your other ankle. See photo opposite, above.

Single hamstrings with band.

▶ Tick-tock (hamstring stretch)

Lie on your back with your legs straight. Place the band around the ball of your right foot and straighten your leg; then bring your leg up towards you, taking care not to bend the knee. Hold this position for three breaths, then open the leg out to the side for three breaths, then cross the leg over your body for three breaths. Return to the centre (leg straight up) and repeat the sequence again twice more.

Repeat with your left leg.

Following the above exercises, perform glute and piriformis stretches as detailed in week 5.

BELOW
Left: Tick-tock; start position.

Centre: Leg open.

Right: Leg across.

▶ Calf stretch off step

This is a simple one – find any step that you can stand on with the balls of your feet and allow your heels to lower into thin air. Hold the stretch for 30–45 seconds. You may find that turning your feet inwards and outwards for a while helps you to feel slightly different areas stretching.

WEEK 10 onwards – complete integration programme

Choose each day which programme you'd like to do, but during the week include:

Hip series 1

Hip series 2

Hip series 3

Spinal mobility or flexicore series (see Chapter 4)

Swiss ball series (see Chapter 6)

Spiky ball releases (see Chapter 5)

Shoulder conditioning.

On all conditioning workouts, if you feel comfortable and confident to do so, increase your reps on each exercise from eight to twelve.

You have the option of choosing to do one workout of 10 minutes per day, or combining two or three together to give you a longer, more intense workout. Just try to make sure you've done at least one of each programme during the week. Remember, input=output, and the more consistent time you invest, the more rewards you'll reap. However, we all know that sometimes, despite our best intentions, life gets in the way and it just seems too hard to fit everything in. If this is the case, 10 minutes two or three times a week is a whole lot better than nothing, and will still deliver clear benefits to you and your horse.

The following are suggestions for themed progressions.

Core progressions from WEEK 5

You can move on to the following progressions (try them in the given order) in subsequent weeks in your exercise options if you are confident and comfortable with the basic one given.

▶ Double leg floats

When you have floated one leg up to the tabletop, exhale to float the other one up to join it; concentrate on keeping your core firm and not allowing any movement in your pelvis or trunk. Float one leg down, followed by the other. Repeat eight times.

Double leg floats.

▶ Toe taps

When you are comfortable with having both legs up in the tabletop position, try tapping one toe down to the floor and then immediately bringing it up again to join the other leg. Now tap the other toe down, then bring it straight back up. You can tap each toe down alternately for eight reps each side.

▶ Single leg floats on foam roller

If you choose to purchase a foam roller, you will find it adds a great balance and core challenge to your workout session. Get used to just lying on it for a few minutes at a time for a few days, then try single leg floats.

Single leg floats on roller.

▶ Double leg floats on foam roller

If all goes well with the single leg floats, move on to double leg floats and also toe taps.

Double leg floats on roller.

Clam progressions from WEEK 5

Try the following progressions in subsequent weeks in your exercise options if you are confident and comfortable with the basic ones given.

▶ Legs up

This exercise is explained by the adjacent photos and captions.

Bring your legs (from the hip) a couple of inches off the floor to start …

… then open your knee towards the ceiling as before.

▶ Clam with band

Tie your stretch band around your knees to provide resistance to the movement. You can also do this in the legs-off-the-floor position.

Clam with band.

▶ Side balance clam

Progress to practising the clam up on your elbow – this increases the challenge by reducing your base of support. To reduce it even further, you can bring your legs off the floor as well, and even add your band round your knees!

The side balance clam.

▶ Side balance – leg abduction

Progress to tying the band around your thighs to provide some resistance to your leg movement. You could increase the challenge further by tying the band around your lower legs instead.

Shoulder bridge from WEEK 9

Try the following progressions in subsequent weeks in your exercise options if you are confident and comfortable with the basic one given.

▶ Shoulder bridge with heel lift

This exercise is explained by the adjacent photos and captions.

Whilst you are in your bridge position, try lifting one heel and then the other without the alignment of your body being disturbed at all.

Progress to floating one leg up while you are in the bridge – this is a great stability challenge and strengthens 'lazy' legs or sides of your body very effectively.

▶ Asymmetric shoulder bridge

From the normal start position, wriggle your feet around to one side a little to put a curve through your body. Practise pelvic tilting a few times in this position, then progress to the shoulder bridge. Work towards being able to wriggle your feet around enough so that you can grab your ankle with your hand – you can hold it like this throughout the movement. I absolutely love this exercise as I know that one of my legs would rather not do as much work as the other, and also my waist muscles on one side are a little work-shy. When I practise this, I can really feel those muscles engage and the shorter side stretch; it is very satisfying and I always feel that little bit straighter on my horses afterwards. Take care that, even though you are in a curve, you keep your hips as level as possible and the weight very even between your two feet.

Asymmetric shoulder bridge; start position.

CHAPTER FOUR

Functional Flexibility

This chapter describes an exercise series which will help you to develop fluidity and flow. After reading this chapter and working through the exercises you will have a variety of movements which, in a functional riding stance, mobilise lines of postural distortion. They also improve core symmetry and strength, lower back and hip flexibility, whilst developing skills of isolation in the upper and lower body. They are based around movements found in Middle Eastern dance, with adaptations to suit the rider's needs. These movements can be practised very slowly and precisely, and it is extremely helpful if you can do so in front of a mirror in order to match the look with the feeling – often, what feels natural is not straight! As discussed earlier, it is often not helpful to force the body to adopt an illusion of 'straightness' when there are deeper issues going on inside the body such as muscle spasm, lack of spinal flexibility/ joint mobility and nerve stiffness. However, because we have taken steps to address possible restrictions in the previous chapters (if you haven't worked through Chapter 2 *please* don't skip it – go back and do so – it is a vital part of the effectiveness of the Equipilates™ programme!), we can be confident that these techniques are going to build on the next layer of mobility and conditioning in your programme, before we go on to core strength and functionalising your body for riding in the next chapter.

In my book *Pilates for Riders* I looked at 'box stacking patterns' and also revisited this concept in Chapter 1. When we want to develop straightness in our horses, simply forcing them into a 'straight sort of shape', whilst micromanaging every footfall with leg/seat/hand and not daring to leave them alone for a stride in case they 'go wonky', does not develop the suppleness required in order to go straight in self-carriage! If, for example, a horse is a natural 'C' shape in which he adopts a right bend posture through the spine, ribs stuck left, loading the left lateral pair of legs), he needs to work progressively through exercises (in no particular order, but all are necessary) which help him to lengthen the whole of the right side of his body, to allow his ribs to swing more over to the right, his left hind to step more forward and his right hind to build more pushing power to drive his bodyweight, and his shoulders to mobilise so he can transfer load easily from the left shoulder towards the right shoulder in order to centralise and thereby plug the 'leak' through his left shoulder. (Of course, if he is bent to the left, all the above applies, but with lefts and rights reversed.)

These exercises work in much the same way. If your body's boxes repeatedly arrange themselves in particular patterns, they can become 'stuck' and resistant to free movement and straightness. For example, a person whose ribcage box is persistently positioned over to the left of the pelvic box feels over time that this position is normal for them – it is their sense of 'centre'. Through first releasing restriction (as we did in Chapter 2) and then practising the opposite movement (the ribcage position over to the right of the pelvic box) we can start to mobilise the chains of muscles which work together to create these postural distortions and thereby increase the possibility of a correct sense of 'straight'. If the boxes in your body are capable of moving comfortably into any pattern of shifting to one side or the other, tilting upwards or downwards, or twisting to the left or right, then finding a middle ground of 'vertical and straight' should not be too troublesome. We can then move on to strengthening the stabilising muscles to support a flexible and supple frame which is not hiding crookedness (as described in Chapter 3). Also, for riding instructors, it is really very useful to be able to cue your clients to adopt certain movements which you may want them to re-create whilst they are actually riding, in order to improve their aesthetic loading.

The first series of exercises in this chapter mobilises the ribcage box whilst keeping the pelvic box still, and the second series mobilises the pelvic box whilst keeping the ribcage still.

Ribcage exercises

Starting stance: standing about hip-width apart with your knees soft. Then imagine your chest is a pair of headlights – lift your chest as you imagine moving the beam upwards onto 'full beam', then move downwards on to 'dipped beam'. Now steady your headlight beam somewhere in the middle, bright but not overly dazzling! Lengthen your tailbone towards the floor – imagine there is a string attached to the very bottom of your spine with a little weight on it, drawing your tailbone towards the floor. If you feel tense, or that the movement is difficult to isolate during any of the exercises, slightly increase the bend in your knees, or, if you are just working on single hip movements, just the knee of the supporting leg: this will help. In riding, although we primarily want to keep the ribcage steady and shock-absorb predominantly in our hips and also the lower back, it is im-portant that the thoracic spine is flexible. A stiff thoracic spine with chunks of the vertebral column all stuck together and moving as one unit means that the correct rotation is difficult; it affects how well your shoulders function and results in an excessive amount of movement being transferred to the joints in your spine where flexibility is greater. The following exercises help to mobilise the thoracic spine.

TOP TIP

You can also practise all the ribcage movements sitting down, to give you the sense of your pelvis being steady, and also your arms still, if you rest your hands on a desk/table in front of you. This also means you can do the movements at work (though perhaps when no one is looking!); when you're sitting at a desk crouched over a computer all day, even doing two or three of each movement every hour or so will help to keep your spine mobile.

▶ Rib slides

This helps to mobilise and stretch the cross-connections through the torso which could contribute to unwanted tilts or shifts of your ribcage box.

Put your arms out to the side at shoulder height. Keeping the pelvis still, reach across with your left arm to the side so that you can feel your ribcage slide sideways – increasing the distance diagonally between your left armpit and right hip.

Now reach across to the right to feel your ribcage slide right – increasing the distance diagonally between your right armpit and left hip. Alternatively, slide your ribcage side to side each time you exhale. Imagine you have a clock face at the front of your chest – you would be sliding the beam of your headlights from 3 to 9 and back again.

Keep your chest absolutely horizontal throughout and facing forward: no twisting or tilting.

You can put your fingertips either on your hips, to check that they stay still, or on each side of your ribcage to check that it is moving correctly.

This movement stretches your upper waist. See photos overleaf.

Rib slides, starting stance.

Rib slide left.

Rib slide right.

▶ Ribcage lifts and drops

Hold your arms softly out to the side – visualise your chest as a pair of headlights with the beam shining out in front of you; keep your pelvis still and don't allow it to tilt forwards or backwards as you do the following.

As you breathe in, tilt the beam of your 'headlights' up so that the spine arches slightly (thoracic spine moves into extension). Keep your head steady and avoid lifting your chin as you do this.

Exhale to 'dip the beam of your headlights' so that your upper back rounds slightly (thoracic spine moves into flexion). Again, keep your head steady and avoid dropping your chin. Think of your clock face again – you are tilting the beam upwards to 12 and then downwards to 6.

You can put your little finger on your navel and your thumb on your sternum so that your hand spans between the two points. Feel how the distance between the navel and the sternum lengthens as your 'headlight beam' moves up, and shortens as the 'headlight beam' moves down.

BELOW

Left: Ribcage lifts and drops; start position.

Centre: Rib lift.

Right: Rib drop.

▶ Ribcage circles – vertical

You have now explored moving the beam of your headlights between the horizontal points (3 and 9) of your clock face and also the vertical ones (12 and 6). Now try to move your headlight beam up to 12, around to 3, down to 6 and around to 9 before arriving back at 12 as you move the beam upwards again.

Take care to keep your chest absolutely horizontal as you move between the four numbers. Now try to move the beam smoothly around all of the numbers of the clock face to create a vertical circle – move as fluidly possible.

Clockwise from above:

Ribcage vertical circles; start position.

Ribcage left.

Ribcage up.

Ribcage right.

Ribcage down.

Place your fingers either on your hipbones to check that they remain still, or on the side of the ribcage to feel how it moves.

Avoid any twisting at all of the upper or lower body.

You can also try placing your fingers on your sternum (breastbone) at this point so you can feel whether it is creating a clear circle as you move. Notice if some areas of the circle feel 'stuck' and practise this both clockwise and anticlockwise.

▶ Ribcage projections

This exercise, as well as the ribcage horizontal circles, helps to mobilise postural distances between the sacrum and sternum if you have a rounded upper back, arched lower back, or both.

Keeping your pelvic box still, as you inhale project your ribcage box *forward* (your upper back muscles will activate) – think Kate Winslet at the bow of the *Titanic*!

As you exhale, use your upper abdominals (your chest muscles will also activate) to pull your sternum backwards and inwards so that your chest caves in upon itself – the sternum should move on a horizontal plane parallel to the ground.

Repeat this forward projection and backward retraction slowly and rhythmically.

Ribcage projections; start.   Ribs forward.   Ribs back.

Clockwise from above:

Ribcage horizontal circles; start position.

Ribcage left.

Ribcage forward.

Ribcage right.

Ribcage back.

▶ Ribcage circles – horizontal

Start with the ribcage on a 'neutral beam' (neither 'full beam'– thoracic spine in extension – nor 'dipped beam' – thoracic spine in flexion). Move the ribcage left (ribcage weight over left foot), move into a forward projection (ribcage weight over the balls of the feet), ribcage right (ribcage weight over right foot) and retract the sternum backwards (ribcage weight over heels).

Then smooth the points out into a fluid circling motion.

Keep your headlight beam horizontal (no full or dipped beam!) and level so there is no lateral tilting of your ribcage box.

The headlight beam should stay facing forward throughout in order to avoid twisting – it can be helpful to imagine that your ribcage box is on a potter's wheel, and is being smoothly taken around in circles whilst your lower body stays perfectly still.

Practise this exercise both clockwise and anticlockwise. See photos opposite on page 80.

Double hip exercises

The following exercises re-create similar movement patterns to those required to sit in the trot and canter as well is turning and lateral work. In order to absorbthe horse's movement in these gaits, your lower back is required to move through flexion and extension, lateral flexion and rotation. The degrees required of these different actions vary with each gait and movement. Playing around with the diagonal and lateral lines of the 'stack of boxes' can assist you in applying weight aids without compromising your upper body position. This series of exercises involves isolating movements to one or both hips and the lower back whilst keeping the upper body still; effective and elegant riders possess the same skills.

▶ Hip slide

This exercise helps to stretch the cross connections through the torso which can contribute to tilts and shifts.

Keep your ribcage absolutely still and transfer your weight from one foot to the other by sliding your pelvis from side to side each time you exhale.

The pelvis should stay level and facing forward without twisting or tilting.

Try to keep your waistband completely horizontal as you move your hips. It may help to bend your knee very slightly on the side you are moving towards as this will help lengthen your lower waist. See photos overleaf.

Hip slide; start position.

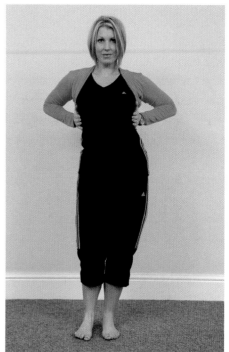

Hip slide left.

Hip slide right.

▶ Hip projections

Keeping your tailbone 'heavy' so your pelvis doesn't tilt forward or back, shift your hips forward so you can feel your weight move towards the balls of your feet.

Now pull your hips back so you can feel your weight move towards your heels.

Avoid any twisting or tilting of your hips or upper body as you move.

It may help to fractionally squeeze your bottom when you first start this exercise, to help keep your pelvis in the correct placement.

ABOVE

Left: Hip projections; start position.

Centre: Hips projecting forwards.

Right: Hips back.

▶ Hip circles

Slide your hips over to the left as in the hip slide; you will feel weight transfer to your left foot. Now move your hips forward so that the weight moves towards the balls of your feet. Next, slide your hips over to the right (and weight over right foot) and then pull the hips back so that the weight moves over your heels, taking care to keep 'the water safely in your bowl' (see tip overleaf) and avoiding tilting your pelvis.

Smooth these four points gradually into a circle – does any part of the circle feel stickier than others? This time you can imagine the pelvic box travelling around on the potter's wheel whilst the upper body stays completely still.

It helps to keep the knees straight (but not locked) in this exercise. Keep your waistband horizontal and your hips facing forward; there should be no twisting.

This exercise has a mobilising and massaging effect on the paraspinal muscles and helps to stretch the lower waist. Notice in the photos how the tailbone stays low throughout, with the pelvis tilting neither forward or back.

TOP TIP

To assist with this exercise, imagine your pelvis is a bowl of water; the water in the ball should stay level throughout so your pubic bone and tailbone should not drop or lift as you move. If you can feel this happening, think about lengthening your tailbone down towards the floor or even engaging your glutes by squeezing your bottom a little bit as you circle. You can keep a hand on your sacrum and one below your navel to check for unwanted forward/backwards tilting of your pelvis.

Clockwise from above:

Hip circles; start position.

Hips left.

Hips forward.

Hips right.

Hips back.

▶ Pelvic twists – standing version of 'push the button' exercise

Keep your ribcage absolutely still and swivel your hips around the central axis of your body each time you exhale; imagine your spine is a pole that runs down the centre of your trunk and your pelvis has to spin around the pole.

Try to ensure that your hips move with an equal range of motion; you may feel more of a stretch on one side in order to achieve this. Working in front of the mirror is important in order to check things like this!

Your pelvis should not move out to the side as you turn your hips. Keep your fingers on your hipbones to check for this. You should also place your fingers just below your sternum to check for unwanted movement in the ribcage.

Your hipbones should stay level and not creep any higher or lower during the exercise, which helps to mobilise the lower spine in rotation and stretch/strengthen the waist.

BELOW

Left: Pelvic twist; start position.

Centre: Pelvic twist right.

Right: Pelvic twist left.

Single hip exercises

Your hips have to adopt a combination of motions similar to those described in the following exercises in the trot and canter. When I work in my studio with my riders, we go into much more detail with infinity loops (figures of eight) in various planes and also undulating movements of the spine. However the subtleties of these are rather more complex and do not lend themselves to be included in this chapter!

▶ Hip lifts and drops

Start by standing with feet hip distance apart, knees soft. Now step forward with your right foot about 6in onto the ball/tiptoes of your right foot. Keep the pressure of the toes light on the floor so that your weight is being supported mostly by your left leg. Your hipbones should be on a level plane parallel to the floor. The slight squat position of your supporting leg, in conjunction with the movement in the waist on the working side and the stabilising muscles at the side of the hip on the supporting side, help you to maintain a good leg position and centred pelvis in the saddle.

Keep your ribcage still and use your lower waist muscles and, to a slight degree, your right bottom cheek to squeeze your right hip upwards as you exhale. Inhale to release it down to a level plane. Repeat this hip lift ten times.

Remember to keep your supporting leg slightly bent and the right toes light on the floor. As you do this, the heel of the right foot should stay the same distance from the floor as if you were wearing an invisible stiletto heel and should not go up and down as you move; only the hip and knee will move.

Keep your upper body (ribcage box) stacked in line above your pelvis; it should not be pushed over to one side.

Hip lift/drop; starting stance.

Hip lift.

Drop back down to the start position.

If you find that your upper body is moving up and down as you lift and drop your hip, slightly increasing the bend in the knee of your supporting leg can help to improve isolation.

Swap legs and repeat.

▶ Single hip twists

In the same starting stance as the hip lift, move your right hip forward as far as it will comfortably go as you exhale and inhale, then move it back as far as it will comfortably go on an exhalation.

You will essentially be pivoting your right hip around your left hip; repeat ten times. Remember to keep your right toes light and your left leg slightly bent.

We don't want your lower back to arch, so you can keep your lower abdominals gently activated (the area between your pubic bone and navel gently pulled in) and your tailbone lengthened down towards the floor.

Your knee will necessarily have to move a little bit, but avoid creating the hip movement by driving forwards/back or in/out with your knee – the effort should come from your waist muscles.

Swap legs and repeat.

Hip twist; start position.   Hip twist forward.   Hip twist back.

▶ Vertical hip circle

Keep your ribcage completely still and use your right waist muscles to squeeze your right hip up as in the hip lift; then move it back as far as it will comfortably go, then drop the hip down as far as you can, then sweep it forward and up until you are back at the starting point. This creates four separate points.

Clockwise from above:

Vertical hip circle.

Hip up.

Hip back.

Hip down.

Hip forward.

Do this again, moving very fluidly this time so that the points you move through create a smooth, tight hip circle. You can put your fingertips on the side of your hip to feel how it makes a circle in a vertical plane.

Repeat ten times. Your left hip may move a little, and your knee will have to move to allow you to create the hip circle. However, keep your ankle steady (wearing your imaginary stiletto heel), toes light on the floor and your heel the same distance off the floor throughout so only your hip and knee move. Swap legs and repeat.

Repeat the previous exercise on each side, but this time circle each hip, to the front, down and then back to create a forwards-moving circle instead of backwards-moving one.

▶ Pelvic tilts

Stand with your weight equally distributed between your left and right feet. Imagine that your pelvis is a bowl of water – without moving your upper body, tip the water out of the front of the bowl (your lower back will arch a little) – your tailbone will lift. Now tip the water out of the back of the bowl – your tailbone will lower towards the ground. Repeat several times to explore the different pelvic positions.

Pelvic tilt exercise – neutral pelvis.

Tilting forward – water 'spilling out the front of the bowl'.

Tilting backwards – water 'spilling out of the back of the bowl'.

CHAPTER FIVE

Releasing Restrictions

Principles of force transfer through the body

We've talked about how one of the most important roles in the rider's body is that of shock-absorption. The more effectively our bodies can absorb the movement coming up through the horse's back from the thrust of his legs without impeding that flow in any way, the more expressive and balanced it allows him to be. The first point of contact in the rider's body that receives this movement – and therefore the forces of compression – is the rider's pelvis.

There is something of a 'domino' effect of force transfer necessary in our pelvic and spinal regions, which in fact continues throughout the whole skeleton. When the phase of the horse's stride causes his back to lift you up in each stride, starting from the seat bones in contact with the saddle, the next 'domino' we reach is the sacrum, followed by the lumbar vertebrae L5, 4, 3, 2, 1, and then the thoracic vertebrae T12, 11, and 10. Once we arrive at T10, our domino effect travels further up the spinal column to the head, but also takes an additional route, which diverts onto the ribs, then the sternum, through the sterno-clavicular joint onto the clavicle (collarbone), and through the acromio-clavicular joint onto the scapula (shoulder blade). When the stride phase is such that the horse's back drops, this all reverses and also flows downwards through your hip joint, femur, knee, tibia and fibula, ankle and all the large, small and tiny bones in your feet, then back up to start all over again. Thus the whole skeleton works rather like a circuit of shock-absorption; restriction around any of the joints breaks the flow. In this

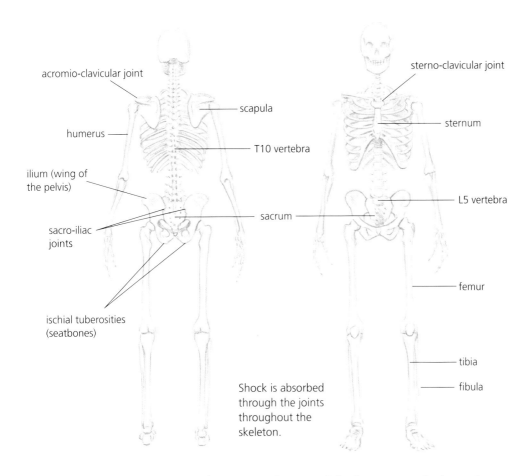

acromio-clavicular joint

sterno-clavicular joint

scapula

sternum

humerus

T10 vertebra

ilium (wing of the pelvis)

L5 vertebra

sacro-iliac joints

sacrum

femur

ischial tuberosities (seatbones)

tibia

fibula

Shock is absorbed through the joints throughout the skeleton.

chapter we'll concentrate on taking care of some of the key areas which need to be free of restriction to optimise the performance of your 'bony circuits'.

Exercises to support muscles involved in force transfer

There are a number of exercises detailed here which not only provide a great release for muscles and muscle groups in key areas of force transfer, but also feel fabulous, and can really help to relieve tired, achy bodies. This is where you will need your pair of spiky balls if you have them, or tennis balls.

Exercises for pelvis and hips

The first few exercises (led in by one to improve stance stability) concentrate on your pelvis and hips: if these areas are symmetrically and functionally flexible, a significant amount of the forces transmitted by your horse's movement can be absorbed here.

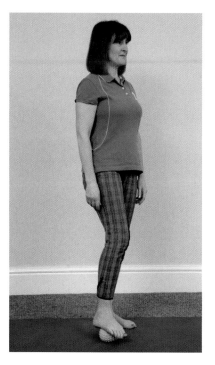

▶ Feet

Giving your feet some attention can feel fantastic. We spend quite a lot of time in Pilates cueing correct weight placement through the feet, but rolling the soles of your feet can save much of this effort before you start your workout session by improving the stability of your stance and helping you to feel much more 'grounded' naturally. Stand with one foot on your spiky/tennis ball. Slowly, and with as much weight as you can press onto it, roll the ball all round the sole of your foot, working around the heel, the arch on the inside, all along the outside edge, the ball of your foot and the toes. You might feel some sore spots – concentrate on rolling these. Work like this for about a minute, and then put your foot back on the floor. You will feel a definite difference! Repeat on the other foot.

▶ Sitting and rolling the seat bones

This exercise helps you to release all the tissues which attach directly to your seat bones, like the hamstrings and the gluteus maximus. It is a great one for helping you to sense your seat bones if they normally don't feel very clear. The sensation you will feel in your bottom after doing both sides is what we would aim for when you are in the saddle – deep and connected to the surface you are sitting on. It is a useful one to try before you ride.

Sit on a firm chair or stool and place one of the balls under your right seat bone. Push your right knee forward and then pull it back to roll the ball back and forth under your seat bone for up to a minute. Then take the ball out and sit back on the stool; how does this feel? Very different I imagine! Repeat with the ball under your left seat bone.

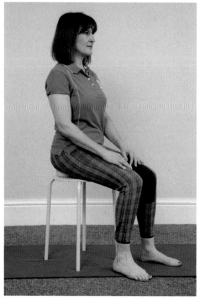

Top: Rolling the feet.

Below: Rolling the seat bones.

▶ Piriformis/glute release

Lie on your back on a mat with your knees bent. Place one of your balls in the area of the right-hand side of your bottom as shown on the photo opposite. Very slowly roll your knees and feet towards the right – you will find quite an uncomfortable sensation in your bottom or side of your bottom as you press onto the ball more and more. That's the right place! You may have to adjust the placement of the ball in order to find this, as everyone will feel it somewhere slightly different. Don't worry if you can't find an uncomfortable bit though; the exercise will still be effective. Roll your knees back to the centre again. Continue to roll your knees slowly on and off, on and off for about a minute. Then take the ball out and just lie back on the mat, still with your knees bent. Again, you will experience quite a difference in how your bottom and lower back feels as this area has released. Repeat, this time with the ball under the left side of your bottom and rolling to the left.

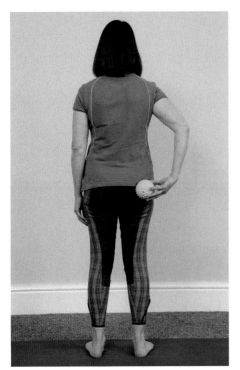

Far left: Piriformis/glute release – placement of the ball.

Left: Rolling the knees on and off the ball.

▶ Hip flexors

Lie on your front with two balls placed in your 'knicker line', where your thighs meet your pelvis at the front. If you feel any pressure or discomfort in your lower back as you do this, draw your tummy button away from the floor and towards your spine. If this doesn't help, try placing a cushion under your tummy (but if that still doesn't help, don't do this exercise). Place your forehead on your hands.

Slowly roll your ankles in and out a few times, then start to lift each leg from the hip alternately just two or three inches. After you have done this several times

on each leg, you can make little shapes with your toes (keeping the leg straight and moving from the hip); circles, squares, whatever you like. Work like this for about 45–60 seconds, then take the balls out and just lie on your front. This aims to release the front of your hips – you'll probably feel a lot more open here now.

Left: Hip flexors – placement of balls.

Below: Moving the leg in small shapes.

Exercise for the shoulders

Lots of my clients really love this exercise, especially if they get achy shoulders, since it really is like giving yourself a shoulder massage!

▶ Shoulder massage

Lie on your back with your knees bent. The two balls should be placed just between the shoulder blades and your spine (not pressing on your spine). You will need to place a cushion under your head. Slowly float your arms up towards the ceiling, and then back down again. Do this several times, keeping your chest soft and your neck relaxed. Now you can begin to draw shapes with your arms (keeping them straight); circles or whatever you like. Gradually make your shapes bigger and bigger, moving slowly and symmetrically. Go back now to just two or three of the floats up and down. Take the balls out now, and just lie back down on the mat. See photos opposite.

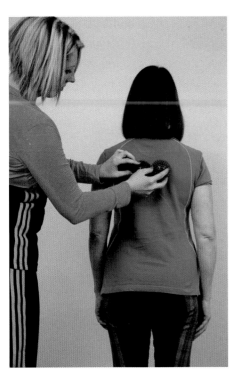

Left: Shoulder massage –
placement of balls.

Below: Circling the arms wide.

CHAPTER SIX

Training Trials and Tribulations

Balance

In this chapter we will first explore the influence of your position as an aid (or not!) of balance. In *Pilates for Riders* I explain how, when we talk about the rider's seat, we aren't just referring to the bottom or the pelvis, but in fact the entire stack of boxes: pelvic box, ribcage box and head box. This means that the alignment of your spine needs to be optimally placed, and to be moving at the same rate as the horse moving underneath you in order to maintain a dynamic balance. At a standstill, your horse's centre of gravity is about halfway down his body, just behind the withers. Once he starts to move, this area is constantly shifting as a result of weight changes and other forces; awareness of where most of the horse's weight is at any moment is crucial to successful training as it gives us a key to his balance. Therefore, we'll call this moving centre his 'balance point'. Your own centre of gravity, at a standstill, is situated about in the middle of your pelvis, but moves somewhat higher when you are riding – and also moves when your horse is moving, so we'll term that your balance point. Get these two balance points talking, and you have a basis for a subtle yet very powerful and effective communication system.

When your horse speeds up, his balance point moves forward, as it also does when he lowers his head and neck; think of a racehorse – head and neck forward and low. When he slows down, his balance point moves backwards, as it does when he raises his head and neck – think of a horse in a canter pirouette – he is active but slow (he's moving, but around, not forward), with high neck and shoulders. His point of balance is much further back than the horse in extended canter.

When your spine moves forward of vertical, your balance point also shifts forwards, towards the horse's shoulders. When your spine moves back again, to vertical or beyond, the balance point shifts away from the horse's shoulders and towards his haunches. It is usually unwise to bring your body much further back than just slightly behind the vertical, and only then momentarily, because of the increased pressure this puts through the cantle of the saddle and onto the sensitive loin area of the horse (the unsupported lumbar spine, which we discussed in Chapter 1 with regard to saddle fitting). On the subject of verticality, permitting or asking the horse to work in a carriage where his face comes behind the vertical for me is a useless exercise and potentially damaging. It is unhelpful to his balance and can easily lead to poor responsiveness to the 'go' and 'stop' signals.

The horse's balance point is further forward in the canter (*left*) than when he is standing still (*right*).

The horse's back doesn't actually move all that much when he is working. His spine does have to move up and down, side to side and to rotate around its own axis in different patterns depending on which gait he is in. However, despite these constant oscillations, the actual degrees of shift between all those points are fairly small in all the regions of his spine apart from his neck. His neck is highly mobile both side to side (laterally) and up and down (dorsoventrally) and later on we'll explore how awareness of how his neck and thoraco-lumbar spine move can help you to train him in a biomechanically efficient way. Meanwhile however, regarding being on top of that spine, the amount that our own bodies need to move in order to stay 'with' the horse's back movements is really only the same amount as his spine undulates and oscillates below us. This means that we don't need a massive range of motion in our hips and lower back, but it does mean that we need to be supple and free of imbalances, asymmetry and restrictions here, which may be magnified when we ride as we try to stabilise on the moving horse. This means that the more our stabilising muscles support us (the ones that both produce and limit forward/back, left and right and rotational capacity), the more stable our own balance point will be on the moving horse.

However – and this is an important point – by deliberately recruiting these muscles very strongly or for prolonged periods whilst actually riding, we run the risk of tiring ourselves and 'blocking' the horse. The horse is so sensitive to tiny nuances of recruitment of muscles or changes of balance or alignment in us that we do him a disservice if we 'shout' with our bodies when a mere whisper will suffice. Purposefully using very strong recruitment of core muscles or those of the thighs or legs whilst on the horse (without developing function and symmetry in those same areas using specific dismounted techniques and exercises), in the hope that eventually this will become automatic, serves to hinder feel and flow, creates a mechanical riding style and limits our ability to find an effortless, balletic sense of dancing with the horse.

Horses often respond very negatively to over-recruitment of the legs or seat as this has a clamping effect on their ribcages, which inhibits proper flow of breath; Iberian horses in particular are very sensitive to this. Developing the necessary muscle groups that we need to support us whilst we are moving (dynamic stabilisers) *off the horse* through the exercises detailed herein ensures that, whilst we are actually on the horse, our positions will be pre-programmed to a certain degree and we can think about maintaining softness and release in our bodies, to encourage a style of riding which centres around nuances of technique and balance, not muscular power.

Contact

The term 'contact' in equitation is interpreted in a million different ways. I prefer to use my (themed!) term 'connection' in relation to the rider's hand with the bit. The horse's tongue is the most sensitive part of him that you have direct influence on. Have you ever had an ulcer on your tongue? How about having bitten your tongue, or your cheek perhaps, while you've been eating? If so, you will be in no doubt that the mouth is incredibly susceptible to feeling the minor imprecision of your own chewing action as injurious to the highest degree. Consider this: the horse, upon feeling discomfort or pain from the bit in his mouth, will engage a variety of mechanisms to defend his highly vascularised tongue, and the bars of his mouth which are covered so thinly with skin. The results are many and varied, from holding tension in the jaw, poll, neck and the rest of the back (imagine how tricky it would be to encourage a horse to go forwards if all the time he feared to move into the pain at the front of his body), to displaying conflict or avoidance behaviour which may be dangerous for the rider, such as rearing or bolting.

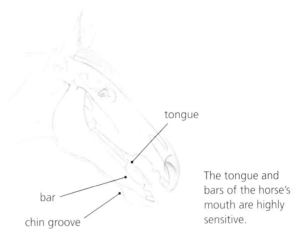

tongue

bar

chin groove

The tongue and bars of the horse's mouth are highly sensitive.

Building a relationship with your horse's mouth using only the most respect-ful use of the bit can open the door to the rest of his body. I will reiterate that he will not perform at his maximum capacity of grace and athleticism if he fears pressure from the bit. Horses who appear to be lazy (if the 'front door' is shut, no amount of pushing from behind will properly sharpen him up), refuse to stop (they 'lock on' to the bit as a protective strategy) or to bend will definitely benefit from the lightest contact possible.

When I train my horses, they wear snaffles and the more advanced ones wear double bridles as well. The snaffle bridles have either a cavesson noseband, or no noseband: we do not use flash or drop nosebands. The nosebands are also loose – the horse has full capability of opening his mouth. I feel that this is very impor-tant. If my horse has a bit in his mouth, it is only fair that he should have the right and the capacity to express his opinion if I am using it in a way that causes him discomfort. If I know that I am causing him discomfort, I can do something about that and improve how I am using the rein contact. If I had a tight noseband and maybe a flash or similar fastened in such a way that he would not be able to open his mouth to complain, then I would be simply saying 'Shut up. I don't care if I am causing you pain; get on with it.' In fact, although I would be concerned if my horse was extremely overactive in opening his mouth in a tense way, or getting his tongue over the bit (again, usually a complaint at the feeling of the contact) I do want him to be able to quietly lick and chew while the bit is in his mouth. If he is able to play with it a little in a relaxed way, the connections between his tongue, jaw, poll and the rest of his spine (not forgetting his brain!) stay open and mobile and therefore I can access the gymnastic capabilities in his body.

I want to keep the contact as light as possible without breaking it. I want the feeling of reins made of cotton, but without loops in the cotton. I want to be able to follow each and every movement of my horse's mouth so that he always feels a light connection with the bit and therefore my hands, without feeling either consistent, jerky or intermittent painful pressure on the tongue and bars of his mouth. For this reason, I aim to keep the feel of the bit more in the corners of his mouth, on his lips. This means when the bit is used, it needs to be used more upwards, rather than downwards or backwards. So, when I want to ask the horse to come higher in his neck to help his balance/slow him a fraction or to lighten the contact, I will use small upward vibrations with both hands at precisely the same moment, and I'll repeat these actions until I have achieved the necessary change.

Bruno is learning to open his frame and work on a softer rein rather than overbending or setting strongly on the contact (it is a work in progress!).

If I couple this with a body aid (lengthening my spine, bringing it a little backwards and firming up my tummy, waist and back) that will indicate to the horse I want a downward transition as well. When the horse responds correctly, my hands stop any upward action and relax down and forward, but not lower than the line of his mouth (or the bit will press on his tongue and bars).

Since we know that the neck is highly influential to the horse's balance, it is helpful to ask him to learn to steady it for short periods of time, which will help your control of his shoulders and therefore his straightness.

When you are in walk, and progressively trot, imagine that your horse has a glass of your favourite liquor on the top of his poll. In the walk, this glass will move slightly forward and back and a little up and down with the natural motion of his spine in this gait – you need to follow this little motion with your hands in order to maintain a consistent light connection with his mouth. However, it shouldn't move, jerk or snatch so much that he would spill your drink! Try to ask him to carry his head in a natural position – not really round at this stage – so that his poll is level with a line about an inch below your navel. He should be very light in your hand, so if he isn't, ask with small upward vibrations for him to maintain that position for a little while. Remember that once you've asked him for this position, he should maintain it without constant aiding, and your hands should not be permanently carried higher than a line running from your elbow to the bit. Make sure you return your hands quietly to a neutral position; give him the opportunity for self-carriage.

If he drops his head, leans or accelerates, repeat your upward vibrations, halt, then release your reins completely. You may need to go quite slowly to start with for him to be able to balance without leaning. Slow, however, does not mean lazy; if you touch him with your leg, he should instantly be reactive with a clear forward response. We can use the same visualisation in trot, but remember that in canter the natural motion of his body requires that you follow the slight up/down/forward/back movement of his head on every stride. Therefore, in order that he doesn't get a little jab in the mouth each time he takes a step, your hands should not stay absolutely still in the canter, but instead allow the motion of his neck to move your hands and elbows a little. When your horse has maintained this balance and light contact for a little while in each gait, move on to suppling exercises and neck lengthening, which are detailed more in Chapter 10.

Contact and balance combined

Let's look at how we can use this awareness of balance points within you and your horse in the rising trot for instance. So many people have a misconception of how they should be positioned in the rising trot; there is a different balance required from that of other gaits. The rising trot should relieve the horse's back by the rider transferring the weight a little in front of the vertical and facilitating easy motion forwards by moving their balance point in this direction. This encourages the horse to also move his balance point forward to keep the rider's weight in the easiest place for him to carry. We use the rising trot in a light seat on young horses and yet often change our balance considerably as the horse's training progresses. Sometimes this change in balance can be detrimental to the horse.

Having the rider positioned too far forward of vertical causes the horse to rush to 'catch the weight'. If the rider is in a very upright posture, with a rounded back, or even behind the vertical, this considerably increases the muscular effort required on the rider's part to project their hips up and forward. It also gives a much greater compressive 'sit' onto the horse's back and drives it downwards, impeding the easy flow of energy from the hind legs forwards through the back, and encouraging hollowness and tension.

Practise the old faithful exercise of standing in your stirrups for some strides as you trot, allowing the movement to be absorbed through all of your leg joints including your ankles and knees. Gradually and softly return to rising but using as

Above: Can your horse maintain a steady balance for a short while without spilling your imaginary drink?

Below: Being too far forward of vertical can compound a horse's tendency to rush onto the forehand in an attempt to 'catch' the rider's weight. It can cause hollowing too.

little effort as possible to project yourself up through the hips. Imagine the top of your saddle is made of Plasticine; you are aiming to leave a very light imprint of your breeches on the top, not a crater! Think about keeping your spine long from tailbone to head *and* from pubic bone to nose; although we want a slight forward incline in the rising trot, we don't want a collapsed front. When you feel as tall as possible, hinge from your hip joints to take your spine forward a little – it may feel as though your bottom is pushing back fractionally if you are doing this correctly. When you land in the 'sit' section of the rising trot, this should feel very soft on the saddle and you should land towards the front part of your seat bones rather than the back of your seat bones or the very padded part of your bottom. If you are unsure which part is which, roll your tummy button forwards towards the horse's ears while you are in halt. If your pelvis was a bowl of water, the water would spill out of the front of the bowl onto the pommel of the saddle at this point. This is the front of your seat bones. You'll feel the same part of the seat bones if you sit tall again and, without rolling your tummy button forward, simply fold at the hips a little to take your whole spine fractionally in front of the vertical; this is the feeling

Left and below: This sequence shows the rider sitting too upright and driving upwards (and downwards!) with her hips. Her horse does not look thrilled.

Right and below: This is much better – a slight forward incline through a lengthened spine helps the rider to be much softer and her horse to move much more comfortably.

you want. If you now roll your imaginary pelvic bowl of water backwards so that the water would spill onto the cantle of the saddle as your tailbone moves down, you'll feel the back of the seat bones. You don't want to be landing on this part of your bottom, as it places you behind the horse's movement.

You may find that if you rise quietly to your horse's trot and allow the muscles around your hips and back to feel soft, he slows down. This would show that he in fact uses an exaggerated seat movement as a cue to keep him going forwards; if this happens, reinforce your leg aids with a quick double tap with the leg, and then a touch with the whip if necessary to explain to him that you riding with an optimal amount of effort (i.e. not too much) doesn't mean he should slow down or stall.

Once you have found that you can rise softly with a long spine and a slight forward incline, play around with the incline of your spine to feel the effects on your horse when your balance point changes. When your horse learns to perform medium or lengthened strides in either trot or canter, his entire frame should lengthen from nose to tail as he increases the stride length through greater thrust from his hindquarters. You can couple a *very slight* cue of increasing your forward incline as you give the reins forward for him to reach into as he lengthens his neck and frame. (Don't exaggerate this or you'll drop him too much on his forehand – only you will be able to tell how much is too much through practise.) Allowing his mouth and nose forward and giving quick taps with your lower calf/heels means he can then learn to think 'extend' not only with his legs, but with his entire mind and body. At first this will create neck lengthening – by allowing extra length you are in fact causing the muscles which pull his neck down towards his shoulders to change in their action. However, when they instead pull the horse's shoulders towards his nose, you get incredible lift and expression in the strides. Over time and with careful training this can help to develop a powerful extended trot and canter as the horse also develops hindquarter strength. Think of how your horse looks in the field when he is showing off – I am sure he can perform a breath-taking extended trot and passage. How far away from his chest is his nose when he appears most spectacular and expressive? Whilst we wouldn't aim for quite that frame when we are riding him owing to the greater degree of longitudinal flexion (him being rounder) being necessary to help him carry our weight, I am sure you can appreciate the point I am making. There is more about how the foreleg and hind leg action are related in Chapter 8.

Remember that your horse is incredibly sensitive to balance and weight shifts, so what feels like 'a little bit' to you can make a significant difference to him. When you want to bring him into working trot again, gently ask him to lift his neck with small upward vibrations on the corners of his lips, and bring your own body into your original slight forward inclination. This will bring his balance point back. Very frequent changes of balance and frame length in this way (each time coupling a slight change in balance through your body positioning along with your aids to increase/decrease the pace), interspersed with transitions up and down between gaits and also into halt, provide an excellent basis for developing the horse's strength and flexibility. At first, increasing the pace may well include a change of tempo, stride length and therefore speed. However, as training progresses and the horse develops greater strength and balance, he will be able to increase and decrease stride length in a consistent tempo. The key is to make these changes at the necessary times – if at any point the horse feels as if he is running, leaning, stiffening on the reins, or he is difficult to bend or turn, his balance point is probably too far forward to execute your request easily. You will have more success if you lift his neck, adjust your own position back a little (but not behind the vertical, or only fractionally if you really need to make a point) and thus relieve his shoulders of some weight. Having less weight on the forehand makes him much more mobile in the shoulders and therefore easier to bend (there's more about how bend and shoulder weighting are related in Chapter 10).

In order to effect the necessary change of balance, you may have to bring the horse to a halt, or even a rein-back, and start again! Remember that, in order to achieve the required balance change by using the rein-back, his neck should not be too low – aim to position his neck so that his poll is level with a point somewhere between your pubic bone and navel. If his neck or poll is very low you won't recruit the necessary muscles to effect an improvement. If your horse feels 'sticky', 'stuck' or reluctant to go forward, as well as checking that his 'go' response is working with your leg/whip (see Chapter 7), it is also useful to take your balance point forwards and begin to offer the rein in order to encourage a neck (and therefore whole spine) lengthening and an increase in forward motion and balance. Each time you ask your horse to lengthen his frame, that process should increase swing, relaxation and desire to go forward. Each time you alter the balance to a higher frame, that should increase balance and lightness, with the ability to slow when asked. After you've changed between different frames a few times, you should have a better quality of movement as the horse will possess potentially all of the qualities of a lengthened, lower frame with a neck and whole spine reaching for the contact, and also the greater balance of the higher frame.

When I'm warming up, I'll keep the horse in one type of frame only long enough to establish the frame I want, before I change it to a different one. This means that, once I get into trot, I might ride only one circle in my higher frame before then offering a stretch into neck lengthening, especially with a weak or young horse. He might, though, lose balance quite quickly once he's been stretching for a while, as the weight of his neck will be putting his balance point more towards his shoulders. When he's on the brink of changing tempo or struggling to maintain a light contact on the bit, or wobbling off his line, I'll bring him back up

The rider is in a good balance with her horse in a working trot.

As the rider yields her hands forwards and gives a light, quick tap with her lower calf/heels she fractionally changes her balance point; this encourages the horse to lengthen the neck and take the contact forward and down, as well to move freely with slightly bigger steps.

again. I won't expect the maximum stretch the horse is capable of giving the first once or twice I ask for it, because his muscles need time to adapt to my requirements. Likewise, when I bring him up, I'll ask for subtle changes in his balance point at first.

In Chapter 10 we'll look at how awareness of your weight placement can influence your horse's balance point in his lateral (side to side) balance as well as forward and back. Now though, we'll disperse the fear surrounding one of the most spine-chilling phrases in many a would-be dressage rider's catalogue of movements-to-master …yes, it's the *sitting trot*.

Rider exercises for the sitting trot

I could go into huge detail about all the precise movements required of your hips and pelvis in the sitting trot, but to be honest it probably wouldn't be all that much help. Instead, I'm simply going to take you through a very simple set of exercises on the Swiss ball, which, along with the mounted exercises at the end, haven't failed yet.

Swiss ball exercises

Each little exercise in this Swiss ball series is a stepping stone to the coordinated actions of the sitting trot, but even if you don't feel this is something you need to work on, you can still incorporate the series into your exercise programme as it contains valuable practice of flexibility, balance and isolation skills.

For maximum benefit, practise these exercises in front of a full-length mirror so you can see clearly how your body is aligned. Sit on the ball with your knees and feet about hip-width apart; remember this should be the width of your hip joints (slightly inwards from the sides of your hips), not the width of your entire pelvis. Place your heels directly underneath your knees. Make sure your ball is big/inflated enough so that your hips are slightly higher than your knees.

Sit on your ball with your knees and feet about hip-width apart.

▶ Bouncing and 'swimming'

Lengthen your spine, and then start bouncing on the ball – this is the fun bit! Keep bouncing on the ball for about a minute, at the same sort of speed as a sitting trot. Try to land in the same place all the time and with even weight through your seat bones – notice if the ball moves around as you bounce.

Bounce for a second minute but, this time bring your arms into the mix with some swimming actions: this isn't particularly related to anything on horseback, but is a really quick and effective warm-up. Try breaststroke, front crawl and backstroke to mobilise the different joints and muscles in your chest, shoulders and arms and upper spine.

▶ Rock 'n' roll

Keeping your upper body as still as you can, roll the ball back and forth with your hips. You will feel your lower back arch a little bit, and then flatten as you move. Try progressively to create the movement with your hips, rather than your legs; you may find that the ball moves less when you do this correctly, but your pelvis and lower back move more. You can put one hand on your tummy and one on your lower back to help you feel how the muscles at the front and back of your body work and release alternately. Try to keep the forward/back motion very pure and the pressure between your left and right seat bones. Avoid left/right wiggles, no matter how tiny! Do 30 seconds of this, then break for a few seconds, then do another 30 seconds.

BELOW

Left: Rock 'n' roll – neutral spine.

Centre: Rolling the ball forwards with the pelvis.

Right: Rolling the ball backwards with the pelvis.

▶ Side slide

Now move the ball left and right with your hips, again trying to keep the upper body as still as possible; your 'headlights' need to stay level. Try to make the movement very even between both sides and notice if you seem to move the ball further in one direction than the other, or your upper body tends to tilt as you move one way. Do this until the movement feels even and fluid – remember the fluid bit; trying too hard will inhibit productive and useful practice. You can place your hands on your ribcage as in the first photo of the sequence to help feel that your upper body stays still, or on your hips as in the next two photos to feel that they are moving correctly. Do 30 seconds of this, then break for a few seconds, then do another 30 seconds.

▶ Push the button

Imagine you have a button just beyond each knee. Push your left knee forward to press the button (your right knee will come back a bit). Release it and at the same time push your right knee forward; keep alternating. Your hips will twist a little as you 'push the button', we want this, but you have to be really careful to avoid any lifting of your hipbones as you do so: the movement should be pure rotation. You can put your fingertips on your hipbones or on the side of your hips to help you feel this. Make sure your upper body stays still. Do 30 seconds of this, then break for a few seconds, then do another 30 seconds.

ABOVE

Left: Start side slides with your seat bones evenly weighted and hips level.

Centre and right: Move the ball with your waist muscles from one side to the other.

Push the button – I have my hands placed where Sally is imagining the buttons to be.

Close up of the start position.

Now Sally is pushing the button in front of her right knee.

▶ Rock around the clock

You can also try moving the ball in a circle with your hips, keeping the upper body still. Move a few times clockwise and a few times anticlockwise – notice whether any sections of your circle in either direction feel jammed. Move slowly and smoothly until the circles feel easy both ways.

▶ Heel and leg lifts

Keeping your whole trunk (pelvis and ribcage) completely still, slowly lift your left heel off the floor so that you are balancing on your right foot and your left tiptoes. Replace it carefully. Now do the same with your right heel. Keep repeating until you are happy that your body is completely stable as you lift and lower the heel.

Practise this first with your hands resting lightly on the side of the ball, then later on with your hands in the 'rein' position.

Now, once you have lifted your heel, try to lift your whole leg a couple of inches off the floor without your body changing in balance *at all*. Repeat with alternate legs, progressively aiming to keep absolutely still through the pelvis and upper body. If you find that one hip keeps persistently lifting and therefore short-ening the waist on that side, go back to the exercise where you move the ball from side to side with your hips, and really feel the waist stretching/lengthening as your seat bone lowers into the ball to push it to the other side. Then go back to the leg lift. You can stabilise the waist before you try to move the leg by feeling a slight

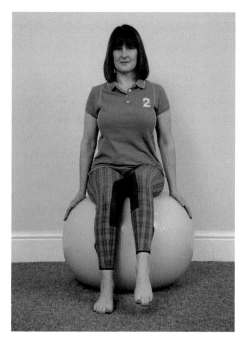

Leg lifts on the ball.

sensation of lowering the seat bone into the ball *first* and maintaining this feeling as you lift. Do this about eight times with each leg.

▶ Let's twist again

Place your hands in the 'rein' position and feel that there are little weights attached to your elbows; they feel heavy. Lengthen your spine; keep your shoulder tops down away from your ears and feel that your chest is open and wide. Taking care to keep your nose in line with your sternum, rotate your upper body to the left as far as you can. Return to the centre, and then rotate to the right as far as you can. Try not to move the ball at all as you rotate! You may only may able to rotate a little way at first but after you have done eight to each side it should feel easier.

Also practise this first with hands resting on the sides of the ball, and later on in the 'rein' position. For an interesting variation, try combining this with bouncing on the ball at the same time.

Far left: Let's twist again; start position.

Centre: Rotating left.

Left: Rotating right.

▶ Bouncing and pushing the button

Now comes the interesting bit: combine the bouncing with the 'push the button' exercise. You'll find that if, each time you bounce, you push the button with alternate legs, each seat bone will do a little scoop down and forward. In essence, this is exactly the movement that each seat bone requires in order to follow the oscillations of the horse's back in sitting trot. Simple, yes? Making small bounce-and-push-the-buttons is similar to a working trot, whereas larger bounce-and-push-the-buttons would be more like a medium or extended trot. Next time you ride your horse, sit to the trot and see if you can notice how he drops and scoops your seat bones a little with each stride – if you struggle with the sitting trot, see if you can encourage that drop-and-scoop motion with each seat bone in turn and you'll soon feel more adhesion to the saddle.

Mounted exercises

Another technique to try, if you find the one above isn't for you, is to change the diagonal that you're rising on frequently in trot, absolutely anywhere around the school on any line or circle. In fact, change it so frequently that you are only doing a few strides in between each change. Do this until you can feel no difference at all in your horse's trot as you change; his rhythm and tempo should stay exactly the same, with no difference in rein contact or balance. When you can do this, you can sit for three beats at a time and then start rising again – bring the changes where you sit for three beats closer and closer together.

When your horse's trot stays regular, balanced and relaxed with you doing this, you can try rising for maybe only one beat before sitting again – then when you can do this on all your shapes and figures, try sitting the trot completely. By this time your horse shouldn't be anticipating any tension and so should stay relaxed, which will make his trot easier for you to sit to. You will also have already absorbed the horse's movement in bite-sized chunks, and therefore piecing those chunks together is less daunting for mind and body. Remember to breathe in rhythm with the trot steps (as discussed in *Pilates for Riders*).

Bruno's very expressive trot requires quite some sitting on!

When I first had Bruno (see photo) I must admit the trot was a shock – he has very expressive gaits and at first it took all my concentration to simply absorb his movement. However, it did highlight where I needed to improve and it was necessary to work harder on conditioning my dynamic stablisers by doing more repetitions and using greater resistance with the stretch bands etc. in the exercises I practise. After a short time, and also doing work to encourage him to move in a more relaxed way, we are getting it together!

CHAPTER SEVEN

Response Training

This concept might be crystallised as 'understanding education and educating understanding'.

The importance of consistency in communication

The next couple of chapters detail some techniques with which you can improve communication between you and your horse. It is so important to be consistent when working with your horse, not only when you are riding, but all the time. This means when you approach him in the field or stable, and when you are handling him in *any* situation. It means that even when you are tired/not in the mood/on a short fuse/deliriously happy and seeing the world through rose-tinted specs, you always give him the same aids or signals, and reward him when he gives you a correct response. This is because anything you do with your horse (handling or riding) is either *sensitising* him to a stimulus, or *desensitising* him. We need to be able to do both, for different reasons. For instance, with the young, unbacked horse, acceptance of the feeling of things strapped round his back and tummy, which seem so alien and threatening, is an integral part of his future as a ridden horse. He learns to accept that these things, while they may be terrifying at first, are not actually going to kill him. The more he realises that he is still okay and breathing after being tacked up and worked in his roller, saddle etc., the more he is desensitised to their presence. The same applies when a rider first gets quietly onto his back. If the horse isn't properly prepared, any slight movement that the rider makes could send the horse hurtling off into the sunset, broncing as he goes. This again, is where a careful process of desensitising (behavioural scientists call it 'habituation') is helpful. When (well before the rider first gets on) the horse accepts in a relaxed way his saddle being wiggled around, the stirrups flapping and banging, things happening above him, the sensation of things against his sides, signals introduced from the ground to stop, go, turn, move his back end, move his front end, loud noises going off in the vicinity, inclement weather ... (the list goes on) it is far more likely that he will tolerate and accept a rider without panic or fear. So, while at first the saddle, the girth, the bad weather and the new sensation of the rider would be likely to strongly motivate him to react instinctively and violently, he gradually becomes less sensitive to their presence and equally gradually they cease to be stimuli for panic.

In the type of situation just cited, less sensitivity is useful. However, to train the horse at all, we do need him to be sensitive and obedient to specific signals and instructions rather than to random things in his environment. The fact that the horse is naturally wary or fearful of situations in which he may find himself in difficulty is why we need to develop his trust in us; by handling him fairly, safely and consistently he learns that we are reliable. Horsemanship practitioners call this being a 'leader'. In essence, if your horse knows that you can be trusted to make sensible decisions about what you ask him to do and the situations you are in, he doesn't have to do all that worrying for himself (looking around for potential predators or threats to his safety); *you* are in charge of security. If a horse doesn't have confidence that his rider or handler will interact with him in a fair and consistent way, he can display or start to display fearful behaviour such as spooking, or bolting or perhaps what appears to be aggressive behaviour such as biting. Such behaviours are often displayed simply to escape or to avoid an unpleasant situation a horse may find himself in; unfortunately for us, after only one incident of it working as a successful strategy for him, a horse will often repeat it time and again. It is remarkable, however, that horses who are prone to persistent spooking, bucking, or biting, for example, can seem to undergo a personality transplant when the approach to their handling is changed. Starting from a place of relaxation and obedience means that training your horse for performance is much more achievable and ethical; it also facilitates sustainability or longevity in the horse as you optimise learning with the absence of conflict and confusion.

At liberty, your horse has incredible natural balance and is extremely responsive to his environment (think how powerfully he can make a transition from halt to canter – even gallop – when that woodpigeon suddenly darts out of the tree near to where he is grazing), and how he passages elegantly when there is a new field playmate in sight. He is perfectly capable of precise balance during flying changes or a shoulder-in along his field fence line. He may also jump a sizeable hedge if he decides the grass is definitely greener in the next paddock! The problems with this responsiveness (and the factors of balance, speed and control that underpin them) become apparent the second a rider clambers atop his frame.

Logic and understanding

Once we choose to do so, it is our absolute responsibility to ensure that we train our animals with an educated, logical approach which they can *easily understand*. Whatever your chosen discipline or activity with your horse, there are some basic educational steps which need to be in place in order for you both to have a clear idea of what each requires from the other. If 'foundation' training is not established before going on to train the horse to perform movements, jump fences or negotiate obstacles, matters can quickly become confused. The inability to complete even some small, apparently inconsequential task, may be interpreted as either an apparent refusal on the horse's part *or* a feeling that you not asking him correctly (as can often be the case with the perfectionist, very analytical, always-blame-their-own-ineptitude type of rider). Perhaps it is something more significant in the horse's training that is a struggle – a particular canter transition maybe; a high-level dressage movement – or something more obvious and potentially more severe in consequence for the rider, like excessive spooking or a tendency to bolt, bronc or rear when under pressure. It could also be that the horse simply doesn't understand the question – hence all the unwanted 'conflict' behaviour is simply a result of confusion over faulty communication.

As riders we can make life much easier for ourselves and our horses by ensuring that we use clear and specific signals to ask for what we want, just as in training any other animal with extreme consistency. In addition to the ongoing study of equine biomechanics, there is a vast amount of continuing scientific research being done around the world which investigates the most effective and ethical ways of training horses, as well as investigations into a myriad of different factors affecting performance and longevity of the ridden horse. A leader in this field is the International Society of Equitation Science; have a look on their website (see Recommended Reading at the back of this book) for more information and updates on sustainable and ethical training. Riders from weekend hackers to Olympic dressage competitors are implementing learning theory principles into their training with great success.

Working with the horse's basic instincts

All behaviours that the horse displays have motivational drives. These include sex, play, food and of course the one we use in equitation because of the intervention of our reins, seat and legs; comfort. When you train your horse, rewards or 'payments' the horse recognizes are rest, food and release of pressure. We need to have a system in place whereby signals are easily deciphered by the horse (not very similar ones to mean entirely different things, such as leg=go and also leg=stop). Each signal always needs to require the same response (leg=go, *always* and *every single time* – not just in a lesson when your trainer is watching, or when you feel really focused and motivated, but *all the time*). With this is coupled the necessity to reward the horse for giving the right response. A horse will be more motivated to give you the right response to your signal time and again if, each time he answers correctly, you reward him in currency he understands! Some systems of training use 'positive reinforcement' which targets the desired response and rewards it; this could be with food, possibly then associated with a clicker, or anything that the horse finds pleasurable, for instance scratching at the base of the withers immediately he gives a correct response (this lowers the horse's heart rate by ten beats per minute!). Skilled exponents of these systems have fantastic results; generally, though much of the work we do with our horses and how we train them uses the system of pressure and release initially, and then we aim to 'shape' their responses. This means we first give a light aid pressure to ask the horse to do something and then, if necessary, increase the pressure to a level which motivates him (this can still be very light!), with immediate release when he does it. He gradually learns to offer the correct response from the first light aid pressure. This is known as 'negative reinforcement'. The negative part simply means you are taking something away (the pressure you have applied) in order to reinforce, or train, a particular response.

When first asking the horse a new 'question', of which he has no previous experience, sufficient pressure is needed in order to make a change. It is also crucial that your timing of the application and increase of motivational pressure is clear: research identifies that the most optimal time in which a horse can make the association between pressure and his response is 3 seconds. Only 3 seconds! If you use pressure lasting up to 5 seconds or longer, your horse may be unable to make a clear association with the movement you were asking for. For example: you are taking the droppings out of your horse's stable. He is standing where you need to put your fork, so you signal towards him with your hand to ask him to move. He does not. You press him gently on the hindquarters. He still does not move. You prod him a few times – he moves. Obviously, as soon as he's out of your way, you stop prodding. In stopping prodding when you have achieved your aim, you remove the pressure. The horse has learned that, after a hand signal which didn't even touch him, he was then pressed, and then prodded. At this point he responded by moving his quarters, and then you stopped bothering him. If this sequence is repeated every time you wish him to move out of your way (and especially if the pressure is applied within about 3 seconds!), he will very soon move away from your hand signal alone – a very light version of the pressure you initially needed to get him to respond. However, if after the first two applications of pressure you applied (first the hand signal, then the pressing) you gave up, tutted at his ill manners, walked around him to the other side and then continued removing the droppings, you will have taught him to ignore your signals which, to him, are now totally meaningless as they amounted to nothing whatsoever.

This may sound inconsequential and of no relevance to your working relationship with your horse, but it is in fact the essence of your communication – however, and whenever you interact with your horse and require a response from him, you must be clear, persistent and consistent. If you teach him that every question on your part deserves an answer, and you can be relied upon to ask questions with achievable answers, he will gradually respond to smaller and smaller prompts (levels of pressure) and eventually seem to be working of his own accord in response to imperceptible aids. Those horse and rider partnerships who give the impression of being incredibly attuned to each other appear so because the horse has excellent associative learning – he has been taught to offer responses to the lightest of aids, or signals, from the rider; so light they are indeed difficult to spot. He is so attentive to the rider that he ignores other things in his surroundings which, without such careful training, might motivate his deep natural survival instincts, which involve primarily flight, but also fight and freeze in order to protect himself.

Attaining this type of partnership is achievable by systematically teaching your horse new things in bite-sized chunks so each tiny part of a movement you request can be 'shaped' gradually. Eventually the separate parts can be combined to create a multitude of complex manoeuvres, giving the impression of the 'happy athlete'. The most effective trainers have a great sense of timing of application of pressure, how much pressure to use, and when to remove it. They minimise the risk of mis-signalling, mis-rewarding, over-signalling and under-signalling. They are diligent enough to always reward the reactions from the horse they *do* want, so that he is more likely to offer that response again. A major factor in improving your horse's rideability and trainability through your sense of timing and feel is to take care not to inadvertently rewards reactions from the horse which are undesirable to you, as he will undoubtedly offer that same response again if it benefited him previously.

Capacity to execute complex movements such as half-pass is built by ensuring each of the tiny steps towards creating it is in place. A blend of go/stop/bend and turn, plus time and patience is required!

Why is the removal of the aids so important? Release= reward. Release means that the horse will want to offer the same response again that came directly before the release, because it benefited him. We've already looked at how this principle works for us in a useful way in a simple thing like asking your horse to move over in a stable. However, it can also work against us if we aren't aware when we are inadvertently giving a reward for certain behaviour …

A great example of the horse who has been got used to meaningless pressure (been 'habituated') and then mis-rewarded is the horse whose 'go' response (see later this chapter) is somewhat lacking – he ignores the leg pressure and will withstand lots of squeezing/kicking/wiggling etc. whilst still crawling along at a snail's pace. The rider touches him with the whip: he goes no faster. The rider touches him again with the whip, a bit harder: he bucks. The rider doesn't like him to buck, so just carries on struggling along at snail's pace, without using the whip again. The horse has been now trained to buck when the whip touches him, because when he did that, the pressure went away. Oh dear! We know that this same horse can feel a fly on his side and his sensitive skin twitches violently to shake it away. We also know that if he was grazing and a gunshot went off nearby or a flock of pigeons suddenly took flight from a nearby tree, he'd be perfectly capable of going from o–gallop in about a second. So what went wrong? First, he was receiving lots of pressure which never amounted to anything, and then he was rewarded for bucking. He needs a clearer system of aiding so that he's not receiving conflicting signals which then become all jumbled up, and also needs his responses, particularly 'go', sharpening up.

Be sure that you ask for what you want, and want what you ask for – don't make payment for 'faulty goods!' (By payment I mean rewarding your horse and by faulty goods I mean unwanted behaviour.)

This buck occurred after Bruno was startled by a pigeon and clattered into the fence. However, if a horse bucks as a reaction to being touched by the whip, leg or spur, immediately removing it reinforces the behaviour (rewards the horse for bucking).

A case study

Having a clear set of signals for the different actions you ask of your horses makes life much more straightforward for you both. Otherwise, how does the horse know the difference? Let's take the following for an example. A rider who was struggling came on a clinic; she had been struggling for some time with collecting her horse into a canter pirouette. She wasn't sure whether he was finding the physical demands of the work too hard (he had had an injury some time before) or was being obstinate and didn't want to do it. Her usual trainer had told her he 'wouldn't take the pressure' of competing at this level as he hadn't got a great work ethic. She had been told to sell him as a low-level schoolmaster who had reached his ceiling and to get a more talented, sharper horse. She had bred this horse and loved him very much. She decided to try another approach, which is why she came for the lesson with me. I could see from watching the horse working for a while that she was using quite a lot of leg to motivate the horse; her leg, even when just trotting around warming up, was fairly well 'on' – sometimes wiggling, sometimes giving little kicks with her spurs, sometimes just squeezing inwards. The horse didn't appear to change anything about how he was trotting, despite the constant interference from the rider's leg. A little way into the lesson I enquired how she asked her horse to go forward from a halt to a walk. She answered, 'with both legs'. The same answer was given when I asked how she went from walk to trot, working trot to medium and extended trot and so on. I enquired how she asked her horse to turn to the inside – she told me she used her inside leg to bend and the outside leg just behind the girth to bring him round the turn. I enquired how she asked him to canter – she told me she used her inside leg to prepare, and then the outside leg, just behind the girth. I then enquired how she asked for travers (quarters-in position). She replied, her inside leg to bend and prepare, and the outside leg behind the girth. I enquired how she asked the horse to slow, or come to a halt and she replied, 'Oh, I never use my hand – I close him up with both my legs.' When I asked which part of her leg she replied, 'All of it.' Finally I enquired how she asked him to move forward again from halt – the reply: 'Er … both legs'. I think by that time she had got the gist of where I was going with my questions.

I happened to know the trainer who had previously worked with the combination and, interestingly, had asked them some time before how the horse knew the difference between all the very similar aids for such different things. The answer, after a pause; 'They just do.' I thought this was interesting, because the trainer in question undoubtedly has that timing-thing down to a tee and probably feels that their horses 'just do' know the difference between aids for a whole range of movements, when in fact this trainer is using slightly different signals or combinations of signals. However, when explaining things to riders and horses who are learning, both find a really simple language of aids much easier to grasp and then build on. All movements, from the simple to the seemingly complex, are born out of the basic ingredients of *go, stop, bend, turn*. We can break 'turn' down into 'turn your back end' (hindquarters) and 'turn your front end' (shoulders). After working on these elements separately within the very simple exercises on the ground contained in this book and then incorporating the same principles into her ridden work, some weeks later the canter pirouettes my client had been seeking arrived seamlessly.

A canter pirouette requires excellent reactivity to the leg aid to 'go' as well as the aids to stop, bend, and place the forehand and hindquarters. These are all taught separately and blended over time to create the balance required for the movement. If something like this is a struggle, the preparatory steps are not in place.

Response to the aids

One more thing … the response to an aid should continue until you give a different aid. You should *not* have to keep an aid 'on' the whole time a horse is performing a movement, simply to maintain it. This applies whether you are cantering a circle or executing a half-pass. So many people use a massive amount of unnecessary muscular recruitment when they ride, because they keep an aid active for the whole time they want the horse to stay in a particular movement or exercise. Again, in order to ensure that your own body is maximally efficient in its own muscle recruitment, and also to enable flow and harmony with your horse, being able to remove an aid *without* the horse stopping what he has been asked to do is vital. A simple example of how you achieve this is as follows. You ask once with your leg for the horse to trot from the walk. He trots straightaway, but after a few strides his motivation changes/he slows or stalls. Your leg and/or the whip need to be used to reinforce the trot aid, preferably to achieve a considerable increase in effort from the horse, and then immediately removed as soon as he does so. If a few strides later he drops the effort again, you repeat the same process, immediately aiding to achieve a marked increase in forward energy (a very large trot or even a canter is fine), but you remove the aids as quickly as possible and resist the temptation to keep him going step after step. It is particularly important for the 'lazy' horse to be very strict with yourself about removing aids in a timely manner and not 'bothering' the horse with them if he is responding well. Interestingly, many of the riders I work with who think their horses are lazy often discover lots of lovely new gears when both they and their horses become more supple and discover new ways their bodies can feel – the equipoise reflexes and postural awareness techniques in Chapter 8 are so useful for this.

Communication breakdown – who is responsible?

Do you sometimes think: 'But he *should* do this … he *knows* what to do … he's just being awkward'?

Here is food for thought: the horse, untouched by humans, is perfect just as he is, as nature intended. Whatever he is now, in terms of temperament, attitude to work – attitude to *life* – is what we have made him, and there is no getting away from that fact. The horse who is lazy, unresponsive, heavy in the hand, untrusting, flighty or exhibiting fearful, dominant or resistant behaviour, is doing what he has found effective to preserve himself and get along in life in his past experiences. If he isn't responding as you want, it is highly likely that you have not explained yourself clearly, either in the moment, or potentially in previous training situations. Imagine starting a new job. Every day for two weeks, you park your car in the same spot in the office car park, next to the entrance. Then you arrive at work the following Monday morning and walk in to be met with your boss, incandescent with rage because you have parked in their spot *again*. Your boss insists that you knew the situation and deliberately defied their authority. However, there was no sign or indication whatsoever that you were not supposed to park in that spot. If you had no knowledge or warning of this, is it fair to be punished? No. A quiet word in your ear on the first day would surely have resolved any confusion before it had chance to build up into an issue.

So many riders feel frustrated and become desperate because they feel that their horse isn't responding how he 'ought' to. Perhaps this is because we are taught that if only we ask correctly, the horse will comply. If he doesn't, we are told to ask harder with more of the same – more leg, perhaps, more seat, more hand! However this is really nonsensical, because if the horse has a fundamental lack of understanding of the pressure you are using – either because he has got used to a similar sort of pressure in the past and learned to ignore it as meaning-less because whatever he does, it doesn't really go away, or he has never felt it before and so has not yet worked out a way to get rid of it, i.e., to get you to stop using that pressure – then he isn't going to respond to 'more'.

The horse only responds (or not) to what you are asking (or not) at the time. He doesn't wait in his stable, thinking up ways to frustrate you that day, or do anything calculated to scupper your training plans.

I am sure we can all remember, or know of, a horse about whom the phrase 'Oh, he's so willing – he just wants to please so much!' applies. Or, indeed, the opposite: 'He is the most ungenerous, sour-tempered horse. He's got no work ethic at all.' Now, clearly, all horses have extremely individual personalities and some can form incredible bonds with their riders/handlers, but I wonder how many horses have been tarred with the 'negative' brush simply because they do not understand their riders/handlers and are thus confused. Quite simply, if your horse isn't doing what you ask, you aren't asking clearly enough. Likewise, the very 'willing' horse has worked out an extremely efficient system of complying with his handler's/rider's wishes virtually before they have asked anything. We could take the view that a horse will not necessarily perform a certain movement or task to please your every whim, or because he adores you, but simply to do himself a favour because he's found, through experience, that when he does it you stop bothering him with your pushes, squeezes, pokes, wiggles and jiggles! In fact, this is the essence of highly skilled trainers – they have impeccable and *reliable* timing of the *release* of the pressure of their aids.

'Pressure' in training

I refer to any sort of question being actively asked of the horse as 'pressure', but this is not necessarily physical pressure. For your sake and that of your animal, having an incredibly responsive horse is what we must surely aim for. The lighter the pressure you need to use to elicit your desired response, the more comfortable for the horse, and the quicker that pressure is removed, the more comfortable for the horse. This means that taking care to develop a high level of responsiveness is not only of benefit to you, but highly rewarding for your horse; a horse-centred approach. It is possible to make *any* horse, yes the big ones, the small ones, the lazy ones, the sharp ones, the downright daft ones – enjoyable partners who offer the best of their ability. It is important to prepare the horse for the questions you are going to be asking of him at a later date; the groundwork exercises discussed later will help to put some of this preparation in place, followed by integrating it into simple ridden work. Hopefully you will be able to continue to blend the simple and easily discernible signals into your current ridden training programme.

Responses – cause and effect

As mentioned earlier, when we train our horses, we aim to develop consistent responses, or particular behaviours from the horse when we give an aid. The aid (or signal) we give to elicit a certain response or behaviour is not a random environmental stimulus like the new saddle and rider mentioned at the beginning of this chapter, but one of your choosing. When your horse understands your chosen stimulus and responds quickly and correctly every time it is given, doesn't offer the response unless that specific signal is given, and doesn't give you some other response instead, then he is under 'stimulus control'. If the opposite happens – you give a signal that the horse doesn't respond to, or he gives the wrong response, or gives the response without being given a signal, then he is not under stimulus control and perhaps lacks understanding of the specific response expected to your signal.

The leg 'aid', when first applied to the sides of a young horse, will more often than not cause him to brace or freeze, rather than to move more forward. Something on an untrained horse's back which touches or squeezes (or even grips) his sides can be interpreted by the horse as predatory – think tiger-jumps-on-his-back scenario. He might try to buck to get rid of it. Therefore, it doesn't give the horse a natural 'faster' stimulus. This is something which needs to be taught, so it is coupled with other types of pressure which may be more effective and which the horse is already familiar with, e.g. gesturing behind him with the lunge whip, or the rider holding a whip to touch the horse just after the leg aid is given. Over time, the horse associates the leg aid with something else coming after it that he would rather avoid – thus, he responds to the leg aid. This process of learning is called 'classical conditioning' and is really the next stage after the pressure-release (negative reinforcement) on the journey to that partnership of horse and rider who seem to have a telepathic communication. This association is also how the horse learns to respond to the 'seat' cues such as engagement of the core muscles, as explained in the section on the half-halt in Chapter 7 of *Pilates for Riders*.

The whip, when used correctly, is actually very helpful in eliciting forward movement from a horse who isn't great on the 'go' response *if* he hasn't been desensitised to it. The problem with pressure-release is that if someone (you perhaps) has applied pressure to a certain degree, but has *not* achieved the desired response from the horse, the horse will then have become desensitised to exactly the amount of pressure used – which is now meaningless to the horse. The next person who comes along (you again, perhaps) and asks the same question of the horse will then have to use more pressure, and perhaps significantly more, in order to elicit any reaction from the horse: frustrating.

It is also very important that the horse accepts the whip without fear – otherwise you may get sharp or unwanted reactions such as extreme speed, jumping away, kicking out or panicking. This might be because he hasn't yet learned acceptance of the whip and is naturally wary, or it could be that, as a result of bad use of the whip in the past, he has become *hypersensitive to it* – too reactive. The good news is that, through systematic and consistent training, old or unwanted behavioural habits can be replaced with new ones that you teach purposefully. When your horse finds that a new, different response benefits him more than the old one did (you'll 'pay' him for the one you want and withhold 'payment' for the one you don't) you'll find he offers the new response more and more instead. The aim of all horse training is being able to achieve a series of learned responses, reliably, in different environments. This means that your aids not only work in your school at home, but out at a competition, or when you are out for a hack on your own; any time, any place.

Establishing acceptance of the whip

Your horse should remain calm when touched all over with the whip. However, when you gesture towards his hindquarters, shoulders or chest, he should offer movement away from the whip in a timely but calm way.

But my horse doesn't like the whip …

In what way doesn't he like it? Does he kick out when you touch him with it, or is he frightened; does he tense up and rush off?

If you don't carry a whip on your horse because 'he doesn't like it' or is fearful of it or bucks when touched with a whip, that can prevent you from achieving certain movements which may help your horse. If your horse is slow or reluctant to move forward from your leg, perhaps into an upward transition, it can be much more efficient to give a touch with the whip after a very light leg aid to elicit the response, rather than having to use lots of leg pressure, which can tighten your body up by recruiting lots of muscle power in your legs, hips, back (and beyond!). Excessive leg and global muscle engagement can, in fact, have the opposite effect on your horse, and rather than encouraging him more forward can 'block' his back and even make him 'body armour' himself against you; stifling the movement instead of allowing it.

The same applies if you are teaching him to yield his body sideways. If you are asking him to move his quarters or his shoulders over with your leg alone and you are struggling as he is just blocking against you, having a softer feel in your body, a lighter, easily released leg signal reinforced with a light whip touch can give a far better learning experience for both of you.

The principle that underlies the following process also applies to other scary things – clippers or a hosepipe to wash him with for example.

- If your horse is seriously afraid of the whip, get him used to you holding it and moving it with slow, smooth movements some way away from his body (a bit like having an invisible 'force field' around him) – have him on a long rope/ lunge line so he can move away but you won't lose control of him.

- If he panics as you do this, reduce your movements a bit but *do not* stop them. Let him move around you, and then when he stops moving, and shows some sign of being interested in what you are doing (standing still, looking at the whip), or relaxing (lowering his head, licking or chewing, softening his facial expression, a deep sigh), *then* stop moving the whip.

- Start moving the whip around again in a non-threatening manner (think conducting an orchestra – slowly!) and when he offers some sign of relaxation stop moving it again.

- Repeat this process until he will allow you to touch and stroke him with it – you might have to use the handle end first. If he jumps away when you make contact, try your best to keep it in contact with his body until he stops and relaxes a bit. *Then* take it away. Do you see how the point is only to take it away when he is already accepting it? This rewards the relaxation and acceptance behaviour. If you take it away when he's fearful and reactive, he's rewarded for fearful and reactive behaviour.

- Repeat these steps until you can stroke him all over his body, starting with his lower neck and shoulders, then his tummy, his front and back legs, his upper neck and head. If he panics, you can backtrack a little bit to an area he was

It is important that your horse doesn't fear the whip; he should let you stroke him with it all over his body.

happy with, but then re-approach the 'panic zone' and remember to take the whip away either partially (back to an area he was comfortable with) or fully (off his body totally) when he offers relaxation.

- You can also make a positive association with the whip by scratching his withers/base of neck or shoulders with the handle end – withers-scratching has been shown to lower the horse's heart rate and induce greater relaxation.

As always, be aware and position yourself sensibly to avoid being trodden on/ kicked. Keeping his head turned towards you is a good idea.

Avoiding working too hard

When we are trying hard to achieve something, it is easy to get preoccupied with just getting the movement at any cost, regardless of how it feels. When this happens, it is common to use too much muscle recruitment and end up immobilising your whole body through trying too hard. This prevents energy from flowing and the movement from being achieved either at all in some cases, or in a graceful and athletically useful way. Sound familiar? Concentrating on making sure you are breathing helps enormously with this, as does asking yourself the following questions.

If I stopped using my leg at this point, would the horse stop or reduce doing what he was doing?

If the answer is 'yes', your horse's 'go' response needs improving – see the exercise to practise for sharpening the 'go' response later in this chapter.

If I stopped restraining my horse's forward motion, would he immediately rush to accelerate without me asking?

If the answer is 'yes', your 'stop' response needs improving – see the exercise to help with this later in this chapter, and the balance and contact exercises in Chapter 9.

And finally, ask yourself:

Am I asking clearly for what I want?

When I get what I want, I am saying 'Thank you, that is right' by giving the horse 'payment'?

Tension blocks communication

'What if my horse is tense and he won't listen to me?' is a thought that passes through many riders' heads. Horses certainly work best when they are relaxed and accepting of their situation. This doesn't necessarily mean relaxed in a floppy, snoozing-in-the-paddock sense, but content in their own skins and in their surroundings. For this, a horse needs to feel safe and comfortable. He may be in a heightened sense of awareness (for instance at a competition), but if he feels safe with you, he isn't in physical discomfort, and you give him something to occupy his mind which will overshadow the distractions of his environment, he can perform well.

On the other hand, it is difficult to teach anything to a horse who is in a state of fear or stress – in Chapter 10 we will look at how reactions in the body are triggered when the fear response activates – you can imagine that when the horse's heart rate increases, and his muscles tense ready for flight/fight/freeze, he is not going to learn a new movement, or even perform a familiar one, in a useful way. It might be that he's distracted, or something around him is activating his survival instincts, in which case it is sensible to do some groundwork (mobility) exercises to concentrate his mind and get him aware of where you are and what you're asking. However, if he's not properly accepting of something around him, or even of you riding him, you can work on the following technique.

This helps to teach acceptance of something scary so that the horse can maintain responsiveness to you even when there is something potentially worrying around. When your horse is approaching something that could be perceived as scary (or something is approaching him), it is *imperative that you breathe*. If you hold your breath, it can attach anxiety around the scary object (breath holding is part of the fear response) and if *you're* scared, then there must be good reason, right? If you happen to be on board the horse and approaching a scary something, holding your breath can make deep muscles in your hips and legs stiffen, which feels like a clamp around your horse's ribcage. This can also be perceived as predatory by the horse. Breathing slowly and quite loudly around a nervous horse can calm him effectively. Don't forget the loud bit – loud enough so that a bystander could just about hear you; don't be embarrassed – be a confidence-giver for your horse. I do this on my young horse when I'm tacking him up, leading him round and in the warm-up ring at competitions when he can get a little nervous – it really helps. As we have already discussed, horses learn through association so, by also being aware of your breathing and making a connection with this in relaxed situations such as grooming him in his stable, you can harness the power of this relaxation association in situations where you need it.

Acceptance of communication – theory into practice

Mounting

One of the major keys to unlocking relaxation and acceptance in the sharper horse is in actually getting on him; this process is an important part of my training and is pivotal in the training of many of my client's horses.

A horse who does not stand still to be mounted, who is wriggling around, swinging his quarters away from the block, or walking off before or whilst the rider is trying to clamber on, shows a fundamental lack of acceptance of the rider getting or being on board. Often, the horse who needs holding by another person whilst the rider gets on to prevent him from moving away can be found to show some unwanted behaviours once the ride has commenced – perhaps rushing, tension, leaning on the rein or refusing to take the contact, or maybe spooking, bucking or napping. Surely even bolting wouldn't be a surprise, as his 'go' button seems to be pressed down already!

In such cases, some questions need to be asked. Is he expressing signs of physical discomfort, or confusion in his work? Perhaps the reluctance to be mounted is his attempt to avoid unpleasant experiences which he may be anticipating under saddle. However, spending time establishing relaxation during the mounting process (no matter how old or experienced your horse is!) can make a really significant difference to how he feels during a ride.

Ideally he will learn progressively to wait quietly while his rider adjusts their stirrups, fiddles with their hat, blows their nose, etc. before moving off *when asked to do so and not before*.

Some clients question why I insist that we go through the following process before continuing with the training session (they just want to get on with it, but often the horse is then tense in the ridden work), but when they feel the change in the horse they understand! It really helps nervous riders to know that their horse is relaxed through the mounting process, as that can often be a huge source of tension for the rider as well as the horse.

- Position your horse at the block. If he won't even stand at the block without moving his quarters away, you'll have to spend time teaching him how to move his quarters *towards* you when you touch him with the whip on the opposite side. You might have to go to the 'quarters yielding' exercise in Chapter 9 first to get him moving his quarters readily away from the touch of the whip, before then standing near his head, reaching over to touch him on the other side of his quarters and asking him to move them towards you. Then try to do it whilst standing at height on your block.

- Rather than just trying to hop on as soon as possible, spend time wiggling the stirrup around a bit – the horse should remain still. If he moves, try to keep him close to the block so that you don't have to jump off *and* you can *continue* wiggling the stirrup until he stands still again. Then you can stop wiggling it, scratch or pat him. Take your time.

- When he's okay with that, try wriggling the saddle round a bit, and patting him on his quarters – again, he should stand quietly. If not, keep doing what you are doing until he stops moving about – and try to stay on the block! When he stands still, stop, and praise him.

- Next, try putting your foot in the stirrup, then taking it out again. In, out, in, out (shake it all about!), all the while with him standing still. Then, put your weight in the stirrup and hop as if you're going to get on, but then stop and take your foot out. Again, all this time, he should accept this in a relaxed way. You can hop in your stirrup and then take your foot out a few more times.

- If all this is in place, then you can get on. By basically breaking down the process of mounting into all the tiny steps that the horse may not be comfortable with, and by ensuring that he's accepting each little stage, there will be no need for him to panic and try to move or rush off. Each time you go through this process, he should be more and more comfortable until eventually all you'll need is perhaps a little stirrup or saddle wiggle just to check he's standing still, before getting on straight away.

- *Once you have done this a few times* and he is already more accepting of you mounting, you can start to create a positive association with this. When you have positioned him by the block, give him a treat straight away. While he's eating it, get on. Then immediately offer him another treat (which you have hidden about your person!) while you're on board. He'll soon understand that standing still by the block = treat, and rider mounting = treat! Do this consistently and he'll wait for his treat before moving – this is very helpful at a show or any other situation where it would be beneficial for him to stay still and calm!

See photo sequence opposite.

1. Remind your horse of the 'quarters yielding' exercise (see Chapter 9).

2. Then ask him to move his quarters towards you by placing or tapping the whip on the other side of his quarters.

3. Now work on bringing his quarters towards you whilst standing on the block.

4. Take your time preparing to get on.

5. Fancy a sweet?

Refining 'go' and 'stop'

Things often seem hard work to perform or maintain if your horse's 'go' or 'stop' responses need improving. Doing so then gives you the time and the necessary balance to work out the bending/turning ones. Have a look at your 'go' response in the 'short-rein' in-hand section in Chapter 9 and try out the following 'sensitising to the whip' exercise

Sharpening up 'go' – correct response to your whip

You can address a lack of forward response, first on the ground and then progressively on board (obviously ensuring that there is no physical restriction which is causing the horse discomfort). If you're riding and you feel you're working really hard to get not a lot; that the horse is not really accelerating when you touch him with the whip, just hop off and do the following exercise. It helps a horse who has been desensitised to the whip to be sensitive to it again. You want the horse to move his quarters away from you, so you can walk a little circle with him keeping his forelegs on the small circle but his hind legs yielding out and creating a bigger circle. This is exactly the same as the exercise to teach your horse to yield his quarters in Chapter 9, but you may have to ask for quicker steps from him when teaching this 'sensitising to the whip' exercise. Despite moving the horse laterally within this exercise, it does in fact help the horse to simply go forwards as well, when you get back on.

When you feel you've made a change (which should take just a few minutes or even less), get back on and you should feel a clear improvement. When you're back on, ensure you help him to learn that, when you ask for 'forwards', the cue of the leg (small touch with both legs to move forward) is followed by the touch, or progressive touches of the whip. In this way he learns to make an association between the leg and the whip, and over time will respond to the leg cue only. If you are consistent with starting using light taps and then making them quicker and more urgent (like at least one tap per second) then sharper if necessary, he'll also learn that light pressure is followed by progressively more, and he can use this information to make sure he responds sooner and sooner to the very first application in order to avoid greater pressure.

- First make sure that the horse is comfortable with being touched all over with the whip – if he's desensitised to it, he probably will be. Therefore just check this quickly and don't labour the point! If he's not comfortable with it – looks tense or frightened – return to the exercise on how to teach your horse acceptance of the whip earlier in this chapter before continuing.

- Hold the reins the same as in the short-rein work in Chapter 9; if you are on the left side, left hand through the bit ring. Be careful only to use upward actions of the bit on the corners of his lips if you need to, not backward or downward ones. Hold the outside rein with your right hand.

- Put the whip more towards horizontal, and 'tap the air' a few inches away from his quarters, is if he had a force field around his body – use the whip on the 'force field'.

- If no response is forthcoming, start tapping with small touches until he moves his quarters – one step at first is fine. The immediately stop tapping and praise him. Repeat this a few times until his response comes quicker. If he doesn't move, or the movement is so reluctant he may as well not have bothered, tap more urgently to provoke more timely and clear steps away – he may need to jump away a little bit. (Tap his quarters, not his flanks.)

- *Be careful: keep his head turned towards you all the time.* The horse who gets disgruntled and would rather lash out against the whip when you ride him is probably going to do so in this exercise too. So, really try to get *him* to step away from *you*, rather than *you* stepping out of *his* way if he gets grumpy. However, keep your wits about you and do not stand in a space where you may be in the firing line for a kick. This ground exercise is often the safer and better way to deal with this poor 'go' response as it prepares the horse for the same principle whilst you are riding and reduces the risk of bucks while you are on top!

- If he does kick out or buck in response to the whip, instead of giving the correct response of going forwards, the whip touches him again; first with tiny taps and then a crescendo of taps until he moves*. *Absolutely as soon as he offers forward response*, the whip stops tapping immediately. If you are very consistent with this, soon you'll only need to put the whip close to his side and he will respond correctly.

    (***Note:** If he has been so desensitised to the whip that he offers no response even with sharp taps, *do not* keep increasing the intensity but instead tie a small piece of crinkly plastic to the end of the whip (secure it well!) so that it makes a little noise in the air as it moves – you may not even need to touch him at all but just show him the whip. In this way, the whip becomes something new and fresh and not just the same old … same old – he is re-sensitised to its presence. Be aware, though; you may get more reaction than you anticipated!)

- As soon as it becomes clear to the horse that bucking does not get a reward (of the whip going away) until he offers a different response (moving away promptly), he'll reduce and then stop it. This applies to other unwanted behaviours too.

Small touches followed quickly by increasingly urgent taps until your horse moves promptly and clearly away from the whip will help his reactivity to it when you get back on board. When he's responded properly, stroke him with the whip to ensure he isn't fearful of it. If you're not confident you can keep a very light feel on the rein when you do this, have your horse in a halter or lunge cavesson instead, so you don't jerk his mouth by accident. (Note: Alf, the horse in the photo, is not untacked for any reason; if you need to do this before riding or in the middle of a ride to help your 'go' response, there is no need to untack!)

Improving 'stop'

If your horse won't stop – or doesn't like to stand still, or is always wanting to move off from halt, ask yourself if any of these scenarios seems familiar:

1. *He's quite heavy in the hand and pulls you forward/leans on the bit.*

In this case, the 'stop' response needs refining. If the horse is leaning, it is most likely to be a balance issue and it is really helpful to practise the short-rein in-hand work to teach both you and your horse about how a light contact in the mouth feels, and how you can work towards maintaining that in movement.

2. *He has his head high and rushes.*

Bending work and mobilising his quarters and shoulders will help him to feel more balanced. And the lateral flexibility gained in the bending work helps him to release tight neck and back muscles; this release allows him to stretch more forward and down (see photo on page opposite).

3. *He just never waits for you – if you lighten the contact, he goes faster.*

If he's always on the go, teach him that waiting for you gets rewarded.

Suppling work for lateral flexibility, as discussed in Chapter 6, helps to encourage the horse to extend his neck forward and down.

I can illustrate this third point with reference to one of my clients. I worked with a mare named Lottie, who spent a long time with her engine over-revving, which meant that any time Sally, her rider, gave her hands forward (or even just stopped having a heavy contact momentarily) and slightly softened her body forward (she was braced back against Lottie most of the time), the mare would accelerate. Any time she was in halt, she couldn't stand still for a second, and trying to teach new and more difficult movements was impossible because any time Lottie was unsure, or was presented with a new question, she would panic and rush off, leaving her rider with no brakes.

Sally had been competing in Preliminary level affiliated dressage competitions, but wanted to move up to Novice. She was really having problems with this – Lottie would either go overbent and very strong in the hand, or stick her head very high in the air and run off. Sally could hold her in some semblance of an 'outline', but only for a few steps, and it felt horrid for both horse and rider.

Sally had tried lots of different bits, a fairly tight flash noseband and also draw-reins. We started by removing the noseband and only using a simple jointed snaffle. We spent time working on the in-hand flexions for lateral suppleness, plus short-rein in-hand work. We've worked with a higher frame and a slower speed to help Lottie feel more balanced, and with a very light contact. Every time Lottie grabbed hold of the bit and tried to accelerate, Sally would ask Lottie's neck to lift with small vibrating *upward* actions of her hands (both at exactly the same time), making sure she released and lowered her hands again after each little upward lift. In using the rein contact upward only, on the corners of Lottie's lips, Sally gave her no reason to brace against the contact and grab the bit, because the bit wasn't being used in a backward or downward action on the sensitive tongue and bars of her mouth. Neither did she have cause to try to rid herself of uncomfortable bit pressure by sticking her head up and running. When Sally asked her to bring her neck higher, this lightened the weight of the neck on the shoulders, thereby relieving the forehand of some load and making it easier for Lottie to slow down.

(If a horse is leaning strongly on the bit it is rather like a crane with a heavy load at full extension – if the arm is too long and too low, it may pull the crane out of balance. Lifting the arm brings the weight on the end more over the base of support and into a better balance. Please note, asking your horse to raise his head to change his balance is *not* the same at all as the horse sticking his head up to avoid the contact and going hollow, which is indeed unhelpful and not good for the horse. If the horse does this, he needs suppling work and acceptance of the contact work, as well as a sympathetic and light hand to build his trust in the bit – see short-rein work in Chapter 9).

If this light upward rein contact didn't have the desired effect of Lottie feeling lighter, more balanced and less speedy, Sally would repeat the upward actions and bring her into halt. As soon as Lottie was in halt, Sally would give the rein completely, as a reward, and really soften any tension in her own body. Often, Lottie would move off again straight away (I had to remind Sally very often to give the rein completely when Lottie halted and not sneakily keep it to cover up the fact that she was trying to rush off again), in which case she had to be brought into halt again, and the rein given. If she did this more than three or four times, we would ask for rein-back from the halt (or, more precisely in this case, a shift back of Lottie's bodyweight). When Lottie offered to go back, we would then stop, and Sally would give the rein. If Lottie immediately tried to go forward again without being asked, the aids for rein-back would go on again, followed by the release when she offered it. This would be repeated until Lottie no longer tried to constantly step forward without being asked. Look at the photo opposite to see how nicely and relaxed she stands now!

Sally has been very consistent about never allowing either herself or Lottie to go back into old patterns of leaning, bracing and pulling. If this happened, she would return to the halt and ask for the higher neck and the very light contact before continuing.

About a year after this initial work, Lottie and Sally are working well at Medium level and competing at Elementary; Lottie is working confidently in lateral movements including half-pass in walk, trot and canter on a light contact. She can also lengthen her neck and spine without rushing or leaning (most of the time!) and perform good medium strides in trot and canter in balance.

Lottie: frequent halt breaks on a long rein reward the horse and create good habits of relaxation and immobility.

TOP TIP

Give your horse frequent breaks within his schooling session in halt on a long rein. It is always helpful to be able to 'reboot' and relax when your horse has done something well, as it helps him to associate offering good work with a reward of rest and relaxation. If you integrate this into your normal routine, when you get into a more pressured environment, maybe a show, your horse will be much more likely to be able to stand nicely when you need to do so without stress. (Think: prize-giving line-ups!)

Teaching rein-back

In the following chapters we'll look at asking the horse to move his bodyweight back and also to step back whilst on the ground. Do this before asking from the saddle, as follows.

Once your horse is quiet in the halt, you can ask him for rein-back by lifting his neck up a little (he will probably need some bit pressure to explain this, but make sure it is upwards, not backwards), then very slightly take your legs back but do not use them! Because of the muscle recruitment involved, rein-back is the ultimate expression of 'stop' – why would you use your legs for this? You need to keep them sacrosanct for 'go' when you want to stop reining back and to move forward again. Continue to give repeated upward (and then release downward) motion of your upturned fingers with your legs back but not on, until the horse gives the slightest backwards response. *This could be merely him shifting his weight back – it doesn't need to be actual steps at first.* Then stop asking and reward him: reins on the neck in halt, or a scratch on the withers, is a good reward. Then try asking three or four more times, each time looking for a clear backward shift of weight. If he actually offers to step back, all the better.

Over the next few schooling sessions, you can repeat your signals, but if he isn't by then offering to actually take a step back, once he shifts his weight back just prolong your aids a little until he does so, then immediately release to reward him. Once he's confidently offering one clear step back each time, you can ask again for another step to make two, and then three, and so on until he understands to rein back for as many steps as you like. To cease the rein-back, slide your legs forward into the neutral position and give your hands forward. He should wait for your leg aid to ask him to move forward, and then respond promptly. I often ask my more experienced horses for perhaps half a long side of rein-back, as it is a really useful exercise to lighten the forehand and increase lumbar flexion. You can really feel the horse's balance has improved when moving off in walk, trot or even canter after doing this.

One step, or even a backward shift of weight is enough to begin with.

Tex – case study of a late starter

My horse Tex (see photo opposite, above) was started 'late' as a 5-year-old, and was virtually unhandled until that point. He wasn't used to the normal things that a very young horse usually learns at an early stage. This means that he had already grown to over 18 hands before learning to have his feet picked up regularly, to be led around in a halter or to wear a rug. Despite having been backed by and receiving his first training from a very knowledgeable and competent person, one day when the circumstances were such that he had a serious 'panic attack' he reared. After this his owner felt he needed to be in a different situation in terms of stabling and facilities, and so he came to me. I knew the bloodline well as I had also owned Tex's full brother Taba, who very sadly died in tragic circumstances when he was just 5 years old. I agreed to take Tex on, but from that first time he reared he perceived that here was a possible escape route from scary situations and attempted to do it on a fairly regular basis when he was unsure of life. Being unsure of me (his new owner), his different living situation, and the questions I was asking meant that, at first, every interaction we had was a challenge. His behaviour could appear dominant and aggressive, but it became clear he was a small, scared boy in a giant neurotic body!

My young horse, Tex.

At first it was a slow process and whilst I was mindful not to put the two of us in situations where we would definitely have difficulties, I started slowly pushing the boundaries of his comfort zones. For instance, if he panicked when having a rug put on and tried to run or lash out, I would rub him all over with the rug then, with it folded, put it over his shoulders and off again, over and over again until he accepted this step. Then I would gradually make my gestures larger and less 'careful' with the rug less and less folded – if he showed signs of worry at a particular stage I would keep repeating that stage again and again – maybe putting the rug on and off six or seven times (or however many it took) until he lost interest in what I was doing and relaxed his body, softened his eyes and maybe started munching his hay.

As soon as he did this, I would stop doing what I was doing with the rug. In this sense, the 'pressure' went away, and he was rewarded for relaxed behaviour. On the first day, I stopped when he accepted having the rug rub him all over. On the fourth or fifth, I stopped when he was happy for me to rub him with the rug and then worked all the way up to carefully throwing the folded rug over various parts of his body from both sides. On the tenth day, I stopped when he was happy for me to work up to throwing the unfolded rug over him in a slightly gawky way with a rustle and shake from both sides. If, on the first day, despite the fact he was very fearful, I had insisted that he have the rug on and fastened up, that would have been unreasonable and probably dangerous (this would have 'flooded' him, according to behavioural scientists), as he would not have accepted in a trusting way that the rug was not going to harm him, or, seeing as *I* was subjecting him to it, that *I* was not going to harm him. By rewarding even a little bit of the behaviour I wanted by stopping on the first day when he relaxed with the rug rubbing over him, he learned to trust that the 'thing' was not going to overpower him, and that acceptance and relaxed behaviour were the way forward. This is why, as the days went on, he readily offered me the response I wanted (relaxed and accepted what I was doing) sooner and sooner.

When first teaching a horse something, whether it is accepting a rug, the touch of the whip, responding to a signal to go forward, or riding a complex manoeuvre, it is essential to reward the *slightest* effort on the horse's part. He will then be so much more motivated to perform for you again. For example, when first teaching the horse to yield his hindquarters or shoulders, *one or two steps* of the correct movement will suffice. When he figures out that one step of whatever it is means you remove the pressure, you can go for a second step, and then a third and then progressively however many you would like. The essence of the solution is in him having confidence to know that in giving a certain response to a particular question, there is always reward.

Again, think about exactly *what* you are rewarding – in the rug situation, if I had stopped rubbing him with the rug when he had scooted off round the stables and kicked out at me, I would have inadvertently rewarded him for doing precisely that. What would probably have happened the next time I had approached him with the rug? He would have scooted off and kicked out. It worked last time, didn't it? When you start to work with the groundwork exercises, make sure you stop and reward your horse when he offers one or two step(s) of the correct movement. If he offers *other things instead*, keep asking for what you want until he offers even one or two steps of it – then stop asking immediately. Remember, he will offer again, what you reward.

Points to ponder

Can you think of any times when you have inadvertently rewarded your horse for doing something you didn't really want? How could you have handled the situation differently to make it clear that wasn't what you wanted? Can you think of any situations where the horse did offer some of what you asked for, and you didn't reward him?

CHAPTER EIGHT

Equipoise – Education in Engagement

This chapter explores proprioception and postural awareness in your horse. Teaching your horse ways in which he can discover useful sensations in his body can really help you in your quest for increased balance, engagement and self-carriage.

Roles of the limbs

We all know that his hindquarters provide the horse with huge pushing power, or propulsion. In fact though, when we see that the horse is more 'engaged', moving in high collection such as a piaffe or a canter pirouette, or starting a take-off for a jump, it is not in fact *just* the hind legs that produce this frame, but a whole-body action in which the lifting and lightening of the forehand is more the responsibility of the forelegs. You can see from the difference in hind limb and forelimb design how they have different roles in force transfer: the angles of the joints in the hind leg means it is efficient in bending and then pushing backwards against the ground to propel the horse forwards. The vertically designed forelimb is efficient in pushing downwards to the ground, thereby propelling the horse upwards. Both the forelimbs and hind limbs can also swing towards the midline under his body and push against the ground sideways, thereby propelling the horse away sideways in the opposite direction. This is how the horse can make turns.

The forelegs are also expertly engineered for a lot of the braking, turning and balance adjustment requirements. We could almost think of the horse having an 'engine' at the front for the forelegs and an 'engine' at the back for the hind legs, whose differing roles coordinate through a specific type of neural circuitry called a 'central pattern generator' to create different gaits and movements. Riders who constantly drive their horses forwards can be putting the horse well out of balance; if the hind legs increase their propulsive power but the forelegs aren't able to match it with a capability to lift the withers up and back somewhat, the horse is simply driven more onto the forehand. Therefore recognising the roles of both back and front is essential. Very frequent changes of balance through altering the horse's working frame and also through transitions are key to developing this fine coordination between push and lift, which creates the impression of a horse carrying himself with springs in his feet!

Whilst the hind legs really provide thrust, the process of lifting the forehand is predominantly enabled by the thoracic sling muscles engaging to enable the forelegs to 'push against the ground'. This is rather like how your arms work in a press-up.

We've already explored the importance of the muscles around the pelvis and hips in your own body, and how the muscles of the shoulders can be affected by hip function and vice versa. Systematically developing the capacity in your

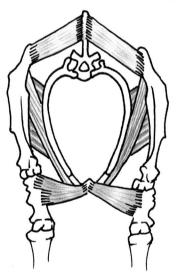

horse to mobilise his body in all directions with specific groundwork exercises helps him to utilise the muscles you'll need him to recruit whilst you are riding him. Integrating these, where appropriate, into in-hand and lungeing sessions can yield remarkable improvements in the horse's posture and movement patterns by helping to increase flexibility, balance, understanding of pressures (which helps with aiding) straightness, and the bond between you. You will no doubt have a good idea by now of movements which you find easy or more challenging in your own body, and how it feels to explore the boundaries of your range of movement, balance and strength. Having an understanding of the physical capabilities of your horse in the same way is useful so that you can devise a targeted training programme to work with the things he finds easy, whilst challenging him to tackle areas he find difficult. For instance, if your horse finds the thoracic lift or pelvic tilt reflexes difficult, he'll probably struggle to seriously engage his thoracic sling or abdominal muscles in ridden work, especially with the weight

Muscles of the thoracic sling.

of a rider on top. You really need these actions and the muscles which facilitate them to be fully functional for optimum performance.

Equipoise exercises

What follows is a selection of useful exercises to do with your horse as preparation for riding him with greater feel (you'll be able to see the horse's body responding and know what you're aiming to achieve), understanding and harmony. Although I am holding Alf in the accompanying photos and the reflexes are being demonstrated by my friend Lisa, a veterinary physiotherapist and McTimoney animal therapist, I usually perform all these exercises myself on my own horses and I advise clients to use them frequently too. I predominantly use the exercises to improve the horse's posture and balance within a lunge or groundwork session, although I sometimes use them on clients' horses while they are riding. I'll halt the horse in between walk, trot or canter exercises and ask for either the thoracic lift, lateral stabilisation, anterior/posterior stabilisation or the brachio reflex. I'll also use these in the stable when I'm grooming, in addition to the pelvic tilt and tail rotation, which you wouldn't be able to do whilst working the horse unless you have someone to hold him. When the horse moves off again into walk, trot or canter, there will be a difference in his way of going as muscle recruitment and postural awareness are improved. I only ask for one reflex response, unless it specifically states that you can ask for more.

Thoracic lift

The thoracic lift activates the muscles which lift the withers and base of neck via pressure applied under the midline in the girth region through the contraction of the thoracic sling and abdominal muscles.

Stand facing the horse's side, level with the girth line. Place your hands on the horse's back, palms down, and stroke down round the ribcage and underneath the belly. Find the groove between the two pectoral muscles (this is a clear dint, or indentation right in the middle) and apply fingertip pressure and gradually increase until you see the withers rise – you'll have to keep an eye therefore on the withers, not your hands! See if they can maintain this lift for a few seconds. On a sensitive horse, once you have got the rise, make your hands flat so you're not irritating him with constant niggling. See photos overleaf.

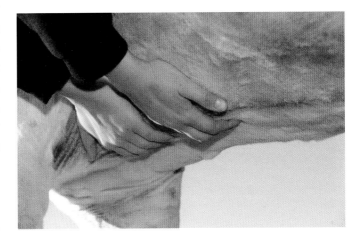

Thoracic lift: place your hands as shown.

Thoracic lift, start position.

Engaging the thoracic sling lifts the withers and chest.

Pelvic tilt

(This is not to be done in a work session unless you have someone to hold the horse for you.)

Pressure applied via the sacrum or gluteal reflex points causes a posterior tilt and flexion of the lumbo-sacral joint. This facilitates the muscle activity required for increased loading of the hindquarters such as in the piaffe.

Stand facing the horse's hip. You'll need to stand as close as possible for safety – watch out for strong reactions! Place your fingers about a hand's width from the top of the tail and gradually and slowly increase the pressure with your index finger – only until you see the pelvis tilt. Then gently release the pressure almost immediately.

Stand facing the horse next to his hip. Place your spare hand on the horse's side and, using your hand closer to the tail, place your thumb at the top of the tail (on the sacrum) and slide up the spine towards his head with increasing pressure for a few inches – until you see the required pelvic tilt.

Above left: Pelvic tilt – hand placement.

Above right: Another hand placement option – for a sensitive horse. Stand facing the horse next to his hip. Place your spare hand on the horse's side and, using your hand closer to the tail, place your thumb at the top of the tail (on the sacrum) and slide up the spine towards his head with increasing pressure for a few inches – until you see the required pelvic tilt.

Left: Pelvic tilt – start position.

Look at the area of Alf's back just behind his saddle patch to see the difference as he responds.

Lateral stabilisation

This side-to-side weight-shifting exercise helps activate muscles of the thoracic sling and is useful in horses who are generally on the forehand, and also to help one-sidedness. It encourages ease of weight transfer through the shoulders and introduces awareness of the resulting changing balance point.

Stand facing the withers and gently grasp the top of the withers with both hands. Carefully pull the withers towards you a couple of inches and then smoothly push away. Repeat to initiate a rocking action.

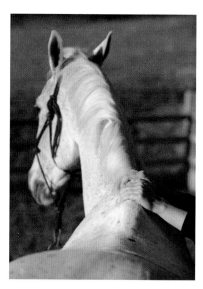

Lateral stabilisation, start position.

Weight shift left.

Weight shift right. Alf's natural asymmetry is left bend; look how he finds moving his withers to the left and moving into right bend more difficult.

Posterior/anterior stabilisation

This works to help engage the horse's abdominals and increase awareness of the loading mechanics of the hindquarters. It is subtle but effective in awakening the deep core. Try a similar exercise yourself – stand up and slowly rock your weight between the balls of your feet and your heels. Gradually make the motion greater so you almost lift your heels off the floor as you rock forward, and almost lift your toes off the floor as you rock back, without being so excessive that you lose balance. Take your attention deep inside your trunk, somewhere between your navel and the floor of your pelvis. You should feel a sensation, especially when you rock back, of a tightening or firming up within your body.

To perform the exercise on the horse, place the flat of your hand on the horse's sternum, fingers pointing down. Gently apply pressure into his chest, aiming towards the tail. The movement required is very small – you should just see him rock back a little on his feet, but he should not move. You can repeat several times before moving on.

Posterior/anterior stabilisation, start position.

Only a subtle shift of weight is required.

Brachio reflex

This muscle has multiple functions including lateral flexion, lowering and some extension of the neck and pulling the forelimb up and forward through its attachment on the clavicular intersection. For this reflex, however, we are going to initiate lateral flexion and a degree of elevation of the base of the neck owing to the additional recruitment of the cervical portion of the serratus ventralis.

Stand square facing your horse's shoulder and have him standing as square as you can. Place your hand on the horse's withers and then slide it down, following the line of the horse's shoulder. About two-thirds of the way down you will hit the top of the brachiocephalicus, which has a gentle bulge. Don't go round so far that you reach the jugular groove. With your thumb, apply pressure into the junction of the brachio and the border of the shoulder. If you are in the right place, the neck will lower and move away from you as the head come around towards you. If you aren't in the right place, nothing will happen! Make sure you are only applying pressure with your thumb, and not your fingers.

Above: Brachio reflex – hand placement.

Above right: Brachio reflex, start position.

Right: Note the reaction as the horse responds. This is a really good one – don't expect quite this much at first!

Tail rotation

This exercise is to be done in the stable.

Gently grasp the dock in both hands and slowly rotate clockwise, then anti-clockwise, to initiate release of the tail vertebrae and increase proprioception of the hindquarters.

Gently rotate the tail clockwise and anticlockwise.

CHAPTER NINE

Connecting with Your Horse

The relationship with your horse is of paramount importance.

Every rider, when remembering exactly how they first got 'into horses', and thinking back to the first times they rode, will recall how they looked forward to the next ride; how they got excited when they got nearer the stables; how they found immense pleasure in being just near a horse, with a horse, and on a horse. This, at the start, was enough – the fun was found in simply enjoying the moment with the horse. As time goes by, we search for more from horses; our goals and aims change. Some of us still find the best times with our horses are hacking through the countryside, whilst others strive to perfect their skills over fences, in the home school and in competition. Sometimes, we focus so much on these aspirations that we lose sight of what initially inspired us so much: just being with the horse. We become more intent on executing movements than maintaining a good, fair and progressive relationship with our partner and friend.

The horse develops trust in a rider who can be relied upon to communicate with clarity, consistency and confidence whilst respecting his body and mind. If we maintain this connection and, whilst keeping in mind a progressive training plan, we also ride 'in the moment', concentrating on the feel, the feedback from the horse and the friendship between the two of us, we are far more likely to access the very best performance in any situation. If you find yourself frequently hitting blockages in your training, this can be very frustrating. Sometimes the same old solutions just don't seem to work. (If you always do what you've always done, you'll always feel what you always felt and always get what you've always got!) The techniques within this chapter have been instrumental in enabling me to move through some difficult times with my own horse and those of the riders with whom I work; try them out and you will see results!

Value and principles of groundwork exercises

In Chapter 7 we discussed the importance of response training and the necessity of ensuring that the horse has the necessary information in order to answer your questions correctly. This information comes from understanding what you require of him – and of course his responses require that he has the physical capability to carry out your specified task. Developing his awareness of you and the body language you use (whether or not you are aware that you are using any!), plus putting in place a 'language' of aids for the separate responses for go, stop, bend and turn, can build an extremely useful foundation for your ridden work. Groundwork exercises can save you hours, weeks, even months of time spent struggling under saddle; a few minutes taken here and there to explain to your horse the principles you wish to integrate into his training, along with the reflex exercises described in Chapter 8, can make remarkable changes in your horse's posture, performance and approach to work.

You may be thinking 'My horse can do all sorts of things. He knows all the basics – he's trained to a high level already – I'm only struggling to get him to do (insert your own movement here!)'. But think: what exactly is it about that movement that causes the difficulty? Would it be better, if only he was quicker to react by going more forwards? Or waited a little more? Or was more supple to bend? Or straighter? Or moved over better with his forelegs/hind legs? If only the responses to the go/stop/bend/turn signals were sharper, such difficulties would not present. Remember all movements develop from a fusion of the basic responses; go, stop, bend, turn …

No matter how experienced your horse, or how experienced you are, if the forthcoming exercises present any difficulty whatsoever, your foundation work is lacking. Improving your and your horse's awareness of body position, application and release of pressure, and the necessary use of the horse's postural and locomotive muscles, will benefit your performance.

If we gesture from just behind the girth line backwards, we'll be asking the horse to move his quarters away from us when we signal using pressure on, or around his body. If we gesture from just in front of the girth line forwards, we'll be asking him to move his shoulders away from us. If we touch him with the whip on the girth area, we'll be asking him to move forwards (initially, when working *from the ground* this will usually be coupled with your reins – we will couple a touch of the whip just behind the girth area with a forward pressure from the halter/cavesson/ bridle to elicit a forward response). Ensure that your horse actually steps forward from the forward signal (and whip touch if necessary) before walking yourself.

Work both sides equally

An obvious but simple step that many people omit in their overall horse-handling and riding (which is particularly relevant to these exercises) is to handle the horse from both sides. How many horses, and people, struggle with working on one rein more than the other? Most do, in my experience. Clearly, it is important to have the horse responsive to your aids on both sides. Surely, in order to achieve this, it is essential that your horse is used to being handled, led around and dealt with from the right side as well as the left. Yet how many people habitually lead their horses from the nearside and never even consider the relevance of this to his apparent lack of suppleness/awareness/responsiveness on the right? If you don't already do so, start handling (and preferably mounting!) your horse from both sides today. It may well feel awkward and clumsy – he may try quietly to adjust his body, or subtly get you to move out of his way so that you are positioned once more on his left, as it is familiar and comfortable for him – watch out for this! Even if it feels strange, put the effort into developing equal handling capacity on both sides, even when in his stable.

Sharp, tense horses

In order to deal safely with, and get great performance from, a sharp horse, you need his attention on you, not whatever else is in his environment. Getting that attention in a way that focuses his mind and calms his body can make the difference between a good ride and a very, very bad one. Do you have to lunge your horse to get some of the fizz out of him? As soon as you go into the school on the lunge line, is he already keen to trot or canter off without waiting for instruction from you? Is he ridiculous when you take him to other places – bargy, or very distracted? Trying these short-line exercises is invaluable for getting him to wait for instruction and to work calmly, whilst giving him tasks to occupy his mind. You can also do them at a show to get your horse's attention on you, when it may not be appropriate to lunge him. Five minutes (or however long it takes) is better spent doing these than rushing to get on a tense horse who may have quite some adrenalin pumping.

Exercises on the ground

Equipment

In the photos that accompany the exercises, you will note that Tex is wearing a rope halter and long rope. When I am working horses on the ground for their own training purposes (i.e. not doing position work with a rider on board) I have only this equipment on, and do not use anything like side-reins, pulley rope systems or anything else which attaches to the bit. This is so that I can get a true picture of the horse's working posture and balance whenever I train him – that is to say, I can see clearly if he is making changes in his way of going as a result of the exercises I choose, rather than simply setting him in an 'outline' for the duration of his training session. This also ensures that the only time the horse feels intervention from the bit is when I am using it through my hand on the rein, lightly and with precise purpose, within either the short-rein work or whilst I am riding him. This also avoids him getting jolted in the mouth by the action of his own body, which could happen in artificial aids like side-reins. It also helps with consistency and responsiveness to my rein actions, as he isn't getting habituated to the bit pressure, which he would if there were constant, meaningless pressure in his mouth. If you work your horse in the same way, with either a rope halter and rope, or a lunge cavesson and line, you'll be able to see clear differences (perhaps subtle at first, but differences nevertheless) in how your horse moves and carries himself after performing the exercises, without you on him. I use this as a great barometer of progress. It also helps me to detect any unusual movement patterns which may point to potential lameness; these could be masked if he was wearing lots of equipment to superimpose a particular way of going onto him.

Basic leading

Your horse should be able to do this from *both sides* equally (not just in the school, but all the time you handle him!)

Walk basic lines of your choosing around the school with your horse about a metre away from you. If he tries to crowd you, or move onto your line, motion him away with your whip, or the end of your rope. Keep your eyes fixed on a specific point and walk steadily but purposefully towards your chosen point – do not deviate from your line at all and especially don't let your horse push you off your line, even if he's messing about or is distracted – you can always give him more length of rope or lunge line, but do not compromise your own line. If he rushes ahead, use short, sharp posterior pressure on the halter/cavesson until he's back walking with his shoulder no further forward than your feet. If he lags behind, use

Walk with purposeful steps on a specific line of travel.

short, sharp anterior pressure and motion your stick behind you until he catches up.

Ask for 'stop' on the short line by using posterior pressure on the lead rope and then purposefully stopping walking yourself – stand firmly grounded by imagining you suddenly weigh 5 tons and are very difficult to move. If the horse carries on walking, or cuts in front of you, gesture or tap the end of your rope, or whip, in front of or on his chest to ask him to go back and wait there so his forelegs are not further forward than your feet – a bit like telling your dog 'Heel!'

Ask him to walk on by using anterior pressure on the lead rope. If he doesn't start to walk straight away, you may need to tap him lightly on the girth area with the whip to motivate him. It is useful to train him to wait for this signal to move rather than just 'following your feet' as there may be times when you need to move your feet without wanting him to move his. Keeping yourself walking on a specific line and not allowing your horse to move you off it, practise stopping and walking on again until he is consistently walking when you ask him to move and stopping when you ask him to halt. You can then play around with changing the speed at which you walk: sometimes speed up and take big strides – he should do the same; sometimes take tiny fairy steps and walk slowly – he should match you and not try to rush on in front or push into you. Practise walking squares and rectangles by making 90-degree turns, keeping the horse on the outside of you but taking care to maintain your line and also keeping your horse about a metre away from you.

Turns

Here, we'll look at different types of turns – turning the horse's hindquarters and turning his shoulders. If he finds moving his hindquarters to the left or right tricky, and certainly if he finds moving his shoulders left or right a challenge, he may be struggling with abduction or adduction of his limbs. Any lateral work requires abduction (legs moving outwards/sideways from his body) and adduction (legs moving inwards towards the midline of his body). Therefore these exercises can give him greater capacity to execute a large range of movement, from the very simple to the very complex.

▶ Yielding the hindquarters

We'll look first at turning the hindquarters, or 'yielding' the hind-quarters. Keep the horse's head turned towards you a little but without him walking on top of you or pushing into you with his shoulders. Motion your whip in tiny circles (as if you were waving traffic past you) towards his quarters – we are aiming for him to move his back end away from you. One or two steps will be enough at first – when he does this, lower your whip and praise him. You could also rub him on the quarters with the whip so he isn't wary of it. If he doesn't move his quarters away from you promptly when you ask, you'll need to tap him with the whip until you get a clear response. Practise this until you can yield his hindquarters away from you clearly and calmly all the way round a small circle – a bit like a turn about the forehand. Ensure you can do this easily from both sides; you will notice that your horse finds it easier one way than the other.

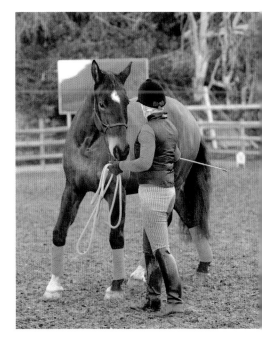

Yielding the hindquarters.

▶ Yielding the shoulders

For turning/yielding his shoulders away from you, it will be necessary to make preparation in the stable (which you can also do with the yielding of the quarters) by pressing or tapping on your horse's shoulders and maybe his neck as well to move his front end away. When he understands this, *from both sides*, start on the short line on a square. Walk a straight line as in the basic leading described above, but instead of making a 90-degree turn with the horse on the outside of the turn, you now want him to be on the inside of it. You can use a driving signal to ask for this until he is really attuned to you: from the withers forwards, the aim is to move his shoulders away from you when you signal using pressure on, or around his body. Have a clear new line in mind at 90 degrees to the one that you are on and simply turn onto it – the horse is likely to be in your way, so keep walking even if it means you bumping into him; hopefully he should move out of your way. If he doesn't, motion your whip in little taps towards (but not onto) his neck or shoulders – sometimes with horses who really don't 'get' this I tap the space at the side of their nose. Keep your whip tapping a few inches away from his body so he can see it in his eye line. If he doesn't move his feet out of your way, you'll have to tap his skin until you get a response. You will definitely notice that

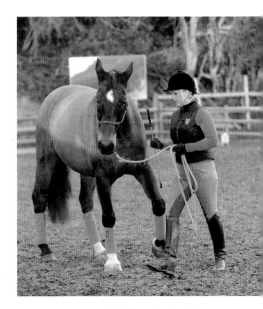

Yielding the shoulders; look how Tex is clearly adjusting himself out of my way as I turn.

his shoulders are either hard to move both ways, or harder one way at least. We are still aiming to keep him about a metre away from you, so try to keep his body well out of that space around you. Remember it is important that *he* keeps a metre from *you*, not you keeping a metre from him!

▶ Patterns and movements based on turns

With these basic techniques you can make all sorts of interesting patterns in the school – squares, rectangles, circles, triangles, serpentines, straight line changes of rein – sometimes turning by moving his quarters, sometimes turning by moving his shoulders. You can lengthen your rope or lunge line out to intersperse faster work – trot and canter on circles as you would in normal lungeing, then make sure you can quietly come back to this work at any point. As both you and your horse get used to short-line work, you can keep a bit more distance between you – maybe up to two metres.

When working on small circles in walk, try turning your whip around and 'tickling' the horse with the handle – tiny wiggles about where your leg would be positioned if you were on him can help him to associate pressure here with moving

his body away a little (shaping himself around your leg), so he doesn't push his body into your leg when you ride him. It also helps the balance between his shoulders. He should clearly yield his ribs away from you when you do this – if not, wiggle on his skin in a more persistent way until you see him appear to bend his body away from the whip and his head towards you a little. If you lengthen the rope/lunge line and make a transition to trot directly after getting a few strides of this, you should see a noticeable difference in balance on the circle.

I notice Tex is falling in to the left on the lunge …
so I use the 'rib tickle'…which improves his balance.

Blending groundwork with reflex exercises

Mix up all the reflexes we explored in the previous chapter with the exercises here. I'll tend to do at least two each of the reflexes (apart from the pelvic tilt, as I can't get around the back of the horse while I've got him on the lunge line!) during a 20-minute or so groundwork session, along with all of the other movements detailed in this chapter in walk, interspersed with trot and some canter. If I see the horse isn't carrying himself as well as I'd like, I'll do a thoracic lift and maybe a brachio reflex, and then walk or trot him off and see how he looks. If, for example, he looks as though he's falling in on his shoulders towards me, I'll halt him, perhaps do a thoracic lift and/or brachio reflex, and then, when I ask him to walk on, I'll do the rib tickle with the whip handle, before asking for trot and then watching for a difference. If he's constantly falling onto one particular shoulder, I might stop him and do the stabilisation exercise to give him a sense of moving off one shoulder on to the other, before moving off into walk or trot. I'd also do frequent turning of the shoulders in walk on squares to move his weight off the heavily loaded one and on to the other.

Backing up

Another very useful tool in groundwork is asking your horse to back up. Backing up not only improves posture, it also recruits the same muscles your horse uses when stopping. Practising backing up can therefore improve your 'stop' response.

Pressure on or around the front of the nose and/or chest should elicit a backwards response. In Chapter 8, we discussed the posterior/anterior weight shift exercise. We need to make the request different when we ask him to back up, so as not to confuse him. In the cranial/caudal weight shift, I use the flat of my hand with the finger pointing downwards and ask very gently with consistent pressure for the subtle shift of weight. When I want the horse to actually move backwards, I'll use posterior pressure on the halter and tap his cannon bones or chest with a whip. Remember that the 'rein-back' is a very powerful tool in shifting the horse's weight backwards, so if your horse appears heavy on the forehand within his groundwork session, asking him to move backwards (at first for just one or two steps but progressively for as many as you want) is very effective in improving his posture. Mix it up in your session and see the results!

Backing up is great for moving your horse's point of balance towards the haunches.

Short-rein work

Short-rein work is another step in transferring the work we've just discussed into your mounted work. With these exercises, you are working directly with the bit – and you can see up close the effect that the contact has on your horse's mouth – something which it is easy to forget when you are at the end of the rein on top. The purposes of these exercises are to create a better relationship with your horse's mouth and to educate him (and you) to the specific actions of the rein and the associated responses required.Until your horse is familiar with these exercises, it is a good idea to lunge him or do short-line work first; if he is very fresh, it can be counterproductive to be asking him to stand and concentrate.

Transferring short-line responses to short-rein responses

It is helpful to practise some of this work before you ride.

Here, it is preferable to use snaffle bits with cheek bars, or Fulmer snaffles, to help the horse to understand the turning aids. Whilst using a lifting hand or an opening rein, the bar removes the risk of the bit sliding through the horse's mouth; the bar also puts a little pressure against the side of his face, which helps to *push* him in the desired direction rather than *pulling* him. However, with these bits there is a risk of the bar getting stuck under the noseband and therefore I will often work the horse at home without a noseband. Once the horse understands the actions of the bit and is responsive to more subtle applications of signals, I swap to a snaffle without bars and a cavesson noseband, which can be used in dressage competitions.

Jaw release

The first, very important, exercise is the jaw release. It is useful to repeat this very regularly, certainly before every ride, as it helps the horse to associate the bit with yielding his jaw, slightly opening the mouth and playing with the bit in a relaxed way as he feels you take a 'contact' with it. I mentioned in Chapter 6 that the aim is to keep the contact of the bit on the corners of the horse's lips, which requires the bit lifting a little in the mouth rather than jamming down on the tongue or the bars. The aim is to teach an association of the sensation of the bit lifting in the mouth (which is what would happen when you take up the reins) with relaxing, licking and chewing. As mentioned earlier, this relaxed, mobile jaw (not a tense, champing of the bit) keeps the whole of the horse's spine unlocked. This ability to lick and chew requires that there is no restriction of this action, so either have a loose cavesson noseband on, or no noseband at all.

Position yourself in front of the horse; he should be standing square, or at least square with his forefeet. Ensure his head and neck are very straight; lift his head either with the noseband or with gentle upward vibrations on the bit rings; you need his head to be a few inches higher than his withers. Place your thumbs through the bit rings, with your fingers relaxed. Push the bit upwards gently towards his ears so that the cheekpieces go saggy; up, not back. The aim is for him to open his mouth a little when you do this, and to start to lick gently, chew quietly, or suck on the bit like a lollipop. If he doesn't understand you can play *upwards* with the bit a little more vigorously until he responds. If you repeat this regularly, he will soon lick, chew or suck as soon as you lift the bit lightly.

Note: all we want him to do is yield his jaw. If he pushes his head towards you, tries to dive down or move his head to the side, patiently but persistently return him to the original position and start again. He should definitely not lean on the bit – we want him to come lighter, and perhaps a tiny bit higher in his carriage, if anything. If he does feel as though he's leaning on the bit or getting heavier at all, vibrate the bit upwards clearly until he stops and feels lighter again.

Above left: Mobilising the jaw, start position.

Above: Lifting the bit into the corners of the lips to provoke licking, soft chewing or 'tasting' of the bit.

Flexions

Now try asking him to perform a lateral flexion – good flexibility in his neck to both sides in this exercise works a bit like carrot stretches, except the bonus is that he can associate the suppleness with the bit, and so you can train him to bend his neck as much as you want from the lightest touch of the rein when you are riding him. Most horses will have difficulty bending in one direction more than the other; this is usually the opposite way to their natural asymmetry. This involves a number of factors, but for our purposes we will work with the two factors of the neck muscles on the inside of their natural bend being more reluctant to stretch, and also the balance between the shoulders. If we have influence over the neck, we have influence over the horse as its role is so important in balance. Seriously suppling the neck helps to stretch it in such a way that the horse naturally wants to seek the bit and work in a round outline. Doing it this way ensures that he does that, but on a light contact too.

The neck is really the only part of the horse's spine that has any significant lateral mobility: all the time people spend thinking they are bending the horse's body is rather farcical, as the horse's spine, especially the area under the rider's inside leg, cannot bend! The illusion of bend is created through shoulder weighting, rotation and the level of abduction of the horse's legs, which allows the ribcage to swing away. The ironic thing is that the part that can actually bend (the neck) people are obsessive about keeping straight, in case it makes the horse fall in/out through the shoulders. This can, indeed, occur if proper shoulder control is lacking. In reality, we can have control over both the amount of bend in the neck (we can use this to our advantage to create release, relaxation and suppleness) and also precise control over the shoulders. This is discussed further in Chapter 10 – for now, let's see how your horse finds left and right mobility.

Stand at the left side of your horse (although it doesn't actually matter which side you start with – this is just for the sake of explanation), putting the first two fingers of your left hand upwards through the bit ring and holding a light contact on the outside rein near the base of his neck. Use upward vibrations of the bit ring on the corner of his lips if necessary to lift his head so his poll is a few inches higher than his withers, as if his attention were mildly caught with something interesting in the distance, but not so much so that he would be frightened of it. It is now important that you remember the visualisation of the glass of liquor on top of his poll now that we introduced in Chapter 6. Slowly push his face away from you and walk with small steps (not big ones or he might try to walk too) in front of him as you bend his neck – the aim is to bend him carefully to 90 degrees, all the time on a very light contact and preferably mouthing the bit. Don't pull on the outside rein to bring his head round, but take up the slack that pushing his head around will create.

If he leans or tries to lower his head, use your upward vibrations again to bring him back up to the same height from which he started. Your 'drink' should not be spilt, and his poll should stay at the same height all the way through the bend. See if he can stay in this position for something like 6–8 seconds (you might have to build up to this), then release and let him come back straight. It is interesting to note whether he tries to move his feet; this could well be because he isn't flexible enough to lengthen his neck on the stretching side, so cheats by wriggling his bottom around.

Do this two or three times from each direction, noting how your horse reacts to the same question on the opposite side.

TOP ROW

Left: Flexions, start position for bending to the right.

Centre: Right bend with me on the outside of the bend.

Right: When the horse understand this, you can also practise asking for the bend with you on the inside.

LEFT

These are both wrong start positions; take care to start as straight as possible.

Walking straight

Now, we are going to introduce the concept of asking your horse to move straight, or to bend, and then to turn, with entirely separate aids. Separating these actions helps you to judge where your horse's balance is, and will also prevent him from anticipating changes of direction, which can result in falling in or falling out from his line of travel. A horse who always starts to turn his shoulders immediately he increases his bend will struggle to maintain self-carriage in both lower-level and higher-level movements. If you can prepare the 'ingredients' that you need to execute a particular exercise before you actually ask for it to be performed, you produce a much more organised picture, in terms of both aesthetics and musculoskeletal efficiency. These simple exercises improve your horse's balance and your understanding of where he perhaps finds certain actions difficult, without the weight and influence of a rider on board clouding the picture. They also prepare you both for asking for the same principles on board, so that when you *are* mounted and ask for the exercise he will already have some understanding of the movement pattern.

Stand at the horse's side and hold the reins in the same way as for the standing flexion exercise, with a schooling whip in the same hand as your outside rein. In order for the whip to be in a 'neutral' position, i.e. not actively asking the horse to do anything, have it angled vertically downwards in line with his foreleg. Have his head positioned so his poll is three or four inches higher than his withers (if he's leaning on the bit at all you'll have to bring it higher until he's light in the contact) – if you can play upwards with the bit a little to mobilise his jaw, all the better.

Ask your horse to walk on as we have already discussed, as in the earlier exercise on the rope/lunge line. If, however, he doesn't walk on immediately, tap him with the whip just behind the girth, where your leg would hang if you were on him. It is important to walk absolutely and completely straight; imagine your feet are programmed to reach the end of your chosen line of travel like a guided missile. Take clear and deliberate steps in a metronomic tempo and do not be pushed off course. The aim is to maintain a very light contact on the bit throughout: walk at the sort of speed you'd like your horse to walk at when you are riding him; if he is lazy, tap him clearly with the whip until he keeps up with you eagerly. If he's rushing ahead, pulling or leaning and you feel as though you are hanging onto the rein or hurrying to keep up with him, lift up the inside bit ring firmly with your hand and, at the same time, draw your hand on the outside rein firmly downwards. This should raise his head and slow him down – if necessary, ask him to halt by repeating the up-on-the-inside-bit-down-on-the-outside-rein actions until he is standing still – remember to either stop asking at this point and have a very soft, light contact, or completely give him the full length of the rein so he can relax – this is his reward for stopping and waiting for you. If he is walking quietly and attentively, you can ask for halt in the same way by carefully raising his head and then firmly planting your own feet into the ground.

Practise these transitions a few times so that he walks on obediently at the speed you require and stops easily. You may notice that he pushes his shoulders into you somewhat – disallow this by wriggling the top of your whip into his shoulder or giving taps on his shoulder with it to keep him away from you and also to keep him absolutely and completely straight.

Above: Walk with purposeful and deliberate steps, taking care to have a clear direction of travel and keeping the horse very straight.

Above: If the horse pulls, leans or rushes, raise his head to ask him to lighten the contact and rebalance, then release.

This is better.

Bend his neck towards you whist keeping his body on the same straight line as you walk.

Walking with bend

When your horse understands the requirement to walk and halt very straight, start to ask him to bend his neck towards you but with little upward vibrations on the inside bit ring – you'll already have primed his muscles for this with the lateral flexion exercise. Take care though to keep walking on your straight line – we want his body to carry on straight and just his neck to bend to the inside. If he tries to turn into you with his shoulders, or to push you off your line, ask him to keep his shoulders next to the fence by using the end of your whip wriggling into his shoulder as described earlier while he bends. You may need to slow down in order to achieve this and to re-establish a very light connection with the bit. When he can walk a clear distance (something like half a long side of the school) comfortably, keeping straight through his body but bending his neck to the inside, in a good tempo without rushing or lagging behind, you can ask him to make a turn – either across the school on a straight line, or onto a circle.

Circling

Once your horse can walk straight, and then bend easily without coming off his straight line, turn him onto a circle by simply changing the line on which you are walking, and start to walk on a circle of your choosing. You still need to keep the bend through his neck, but if he swings his quarters out when you get onto the circle you need to walk faster – we don't want swinging quarters. When you have walked your circle with a good amount of bend, offer the rein forward and down to the floor to ask him to lengthen his neck and stretch. After he has done this, it is a good time to bring his back up, halt and completely release the reins to let him have a rest. See photos opposite, above.

Turning the shoulder

When you have picked the contact back up again, try asking your horse to turn away from you – you can make changes of rein like this, or maybe walking through serpentines or squares. You can either push him into a bend away from you and then turn your feet to change your direction of travel by 90 degrees so that he bends into the direction of the turn, or keep him very slightly bent towards you as you move his shoulders away from you, so that he actually turns

Once your horse can walk straight and then bend easily, turn him onto a circle.

Then try lengthening the neck by taking the rein forward and down. You can go further than this if you wish.

in a counter-bend. He should already know by now to move his feet out of your way. Whenever you work in a counter-bend (and this applies whether you are working in hand or riding), you need only a very minor bend in his neck; nowhere near as much as you have just been working with for suppleness. I like to think of counter-bend work is more focusing on control of the shoulders than suppleness – think about having just enough bend so that just his eyeballs are looking at you

Turning your horse away from you is useful so that you can change the bend without changing sides. Also, it helps build mobility in his shoulders. In this photo he's bending into the turn.

And this way he's in a counter-bend; bending away from the direction of the turn.

really. Being able to do this means you can work the horse on both reins without having to change which side of him you are on for a while. However it is useful, as we have already discussed, to work him from both the left and the right sides.

TIP – take time to establish correct work

It usually takes a few sessions to work on improving responses and balance, as well as your own self-discipline regarding line of travel, etc. in the above exercises. When you and your horse are confident with them, try the following exercises.

Circling with quarters out

This exercise is one of the fundamental preparatory exercises for lateral work, in that it teaches the horse how to yield his quarters from the pressure of an isolated 'leg' or in this case, a touch of the whip. I prefer this to the leg-yield as a first exercise as there are fewer variables with which the horse (and rider) can make errors – we are simply adding another element onto an exercise the horse already understands. It can also, along with the counter shoulder-in exercise that

follows, seriously improve the angle your horse is able to offer in the shoulder-in.

Once you have asked your horse to bend and then come onto a small circle, keep his forefeet precisely stepping on the same circle line (not allowing his shoulders to come closer to you, nor further away), but now angle your schooling whip horizontally towards his hip, and tap him there to ask him to move his quarters out onto a circle of a larger diameter than the one his forefeet are travelling on. A couple of steps are enough at first, but progressively you can ask for a whole circle or more. Your horse should keep his head and neck at the same height at which you started the exercise, and retain a light contact. If you offer the rein forward and down to allow the horse to lengthen his neck and stretch after doing this, you will usually get a good stretch response.

Asking for yielding of the quarters on the circle is an excellent suppling exercise and preparation for later lateral work.

Counter shoulder-in

You can now try asking your horse to move laterally along the fence line, again by yielding his quarters away a little. This helps to develop power in the hind leg that is closer to the fence, and can assist in transferring weight towards the shoulder on the opposite side. Start by walking straight around the short side of the school, but with yourself positioned between the fence and the horse and your whip in the neutral position. As you come around the corner onto the long side, raise your whip to the horizontal position and tap him if necessary to ask him to yield his quarters away from the fence. Keep walking in a very straight line, always exactly the same distance away from the fence, with the horse bent towards you a little and keeping the whip just near him but in the horizontal position so you can touch him again if necessary. Once your horse is used to this, as soon as he gives you the required position you can bring your whip back towards neutral and only raise it again if he comes out of position. In this way, he learns to maintain lateral positions for himself.

Counter shoulder-in is extremely useful for improving mobility and strengthens the hind leg closer to the fence.

Shoulder-in

Teaching the shoulder-in position in hand shows him the movement pattern you will require later on in ridden work, and also develops power in the inside hind leg and assists with moving weight towards the outside shoulder. This time, walk along the short side with the horse between you and the fence. As you come around the corner, bend him towards you a little for two or three steps, then take one step towards the inside of the school to bring his shoulders with you and then continue to walk very straight towards the end of the school, but bring your whip up into the horizontal position to keep his quarters on the track. Aim to maintain this angle first for a few steps, then over time all the way down the long side – or even all the way around the school!

Shoulder-in is a foundation lateral movement. It is very beneficial for developing power in the inside hind leg as it becomes predominantly responsible for pushing the horse's bodyweight along this line of travel.

Principles into practice …

The photo opposite shows my horse, Bruno. At the time of writing this I had owned him for only about three months, and he had already been competing with some success at an advanced level of dressage in Holland when I bought him. He struggled noticeably with any movement which required him to assume right bend, whether that was a circle, or half-pass, or a pirouette. I noticed that he was a fairly classically 'left bent horse', who loaded his right lateral pair of legs more than the left. In movement, he would protract his left hind further forward than his right; his ribcage seemed to be 'stuck' against my right leg, he would fall/escape through his right shoulder given half a chance, and his neck would much prefer to be in left bend – or right bend, with a head tilt. He also relied heavily on the fact that I would keep him going every step in whatever he happened to be doing.

There were clearly several areas in which I felt I needed to set up a different way of communicating. I started with the jaw release and neck flexions to help him work in a lighter contact and to have confidence to take my rein forward and

Bruno and me.

down. This definitely helped, but the difference in how the hind legs felt was very much still present. I worked through exercises on the lunge (only using the halter and rope) including the 'tickling' exercise, which helped him to feel that he could move his ribcage more to the left, which he had previously resisted. I also worked him through the short-rein exercises, which increased his sense of moving off quickly and also walking with purpose until I asked him to come to a halt. Working on the straightness, then adding the bend, then asking for turning when I was happy that the other two requests were understood, helped him to process my different set of signals. Working a little with the lateral positions (yielding the quarters on a circle, then counter shoulder-in and then finally shoulder-in) began to help him discover his balance and also introduced him to the concept of staying in position unless I asked otherwise, without having to cope with the added factor of me being on board as well. In the reflex work, he was quite sensitive around his tummy and at first would try to bite himself (and occasionally took a nip towards me), but when I asked a little less, and stroked him to get him used to my hands being around that area before asking, he accepted it more and has started to give much better, if small, correct responses. Combining this work programme with physiotherapy to release several well-established patterns of restriction means he is now more comfortable in himself and therefore easier and more enjoyable to ride.

I knew when I bought him that he had previously had problems in his back, and with an ill-fitting saddle; hence I was not surprised when I found that he was very unconfident with the mounting process. Look back at the photos in the Mounting section in Chapter 7 and you will see that Bruno is demonstrating the steps to relaxed mounting. Believe me, this was not merely a case of 'going through the motions' – when I first led him to the mounting block he was terrified and spooked violently away from it. Initially I thought something in the trees had perhaps startled him, but it was immediately very clear when we re-approached it that indeed it was the block itself that was the cause of his distress. The fear in his eyes and the tension in his body were plain to see, and I would certainly have expected him to eject me without delay, had I just insisted on getting on him at that point, perhaps by getting someone to restrain him while I mounted. That first time, it took me about 20 minutes to go through all the steps of getting on. His back did feel tense when I was in the saddle, and I wasn't sure quite how far we would get around the school before there'd be some sort of reaction from him. In fact, though, after two or three circles (I kept him on a turn, with a clear opening inside rein and a very soft outside rein so he didn't feel trapped, just in case!) he relaxed, started to breathe, and was absolutely fine.

Each time I rode him after that, we carefully went through the same process, with me being aware of the need to keep my emotions and breathing extremely calm, and not to show any sign of frustration. Day by day it took a few minutes less to reach a level of relaxation where I felt it was appropriate to get on, and each day the steps in which he felt tense and braced reduced. After about a month, he stood totally calmly and I was able to get on straight away, with a relaxed horse mentally and physically. We are building a good relationship and I look forward to seeing how he develops as our partnership grows.

Important note!

Just to reiterate the point regarding mounting discussed in Chapter 7; if your horse does not stand still for you to get on at the mounting block, swings his body away, tries to rush off the millisecond you get your foot in the stirrup, or always requires someone to hold him while you get on, this for me sets alarm bells ringing. In this situation, often some issue is to be found in the ridden work (e.g. he's very tense/sharp/he bucks/he spooks/he has no brakes). If your horse does not allow you to mount him, without requiring help, in a calm and relaxed way and stands while you fiddle with your stirrups, rearrange your coat, gather your reins, etc. before moving *when you ask and not before,* there is a fundamental lack of acceptance of you being up there on board. This can then manifest itself straightaway through one or more of the above behaviours.

Although some riders I have worked with have at first failed to see the relevance of my insistence upon establishing good mounting patterns before the lesson may begin (and this can indeed take the majority of the lesson in some cases!), after experiencing the difference in how their horses feel and work once they have done so, they wonder why on earth nobody had explained this to them before. Riders, too, who are perhaps nervous or apprehensive of mounting their horse, or a new horse, gain confidence from going through the process of ensuring their acceptance by the horse. Even mounting a horse requires his understanding of the go/stop/turn signals so that you can position him correctly beside a block, and alter his position if he is reluctant to stand where you need him to. Working through the exercises in this chapter provides the building blocks for a relevant language between you for calm mounting.

CHAPTER TEN

Mirror, Signal, Manoeuvre

I've called this chapter 'Mirror, signal, manoeuvre' because it sums up quite neatly the order of things! You and your horse are a mirror of one another's balance and energy, so it makes sense to take a look at the 'reflection' to see what the current situation is in terms of this, before asking the horse to make any change of speed, gait or direction. Take time to assess exactly how your horse feels at any given moment. Is he light in the contact? Yes? Good – you can go on with your exercises. No? Change his balance point front to back and remind him that neither of you wishes to have a heavy feeling on the bit. Do you want him straight – is he straight? Yes? Good, carry on with your exercise. No? Change his balance point side to side. Do you want bend – is he bending? Yes? Excellent, carry on with your exercise. No? Come back to a gait (or even halt) in which he is more comfortable so you can re-explain the bending aids, then ask again. If you get stuck with the ridden exercises, dismount and work on them in hand, before getting back on and trying again. Is your horse responsive, all the time, to the aids to go, stop and turn? You get the idea. When you have assessed how your horse currently feels and you have an idea of an exercise which would help to improve the situation, you can prepare him with the relevant signals, and then execute your manoeuvre with precision and poise! Try the ideas in this chapter to help you communicate clearly the different components of direction (straightness), bending, (suppleness) and turning (mobility).

The system of aiding used involves applying specific aids with separate parts of your body to elicit a particular response from your horse. This makes sense, as it significantly reduces confusion which can occur when the horse receives mixed messages from your body, with you getting frustrated because he's not doing as you want! When the horse reliably understands signals to go, stop, bend, turn, align himself and round his spine, the signals can be combined to give every possibility of movement required. Unfortunately I do not have the scope within these limited pages to explore the aiding combinations for all the movements, but sharpening up your own awareness of the use of your body, and the responses your horse gives to the questions you ask of him, will help you build a deeper level of communication, timing and feel. This results in greater partnership, and better performance.

Organising the horse's balance

In Chapter 6 we discussed 'balance points' in the horse and rider. In order to help organise the horse's balance, we need to be aware of where his energy leaks are. As mentioned earlier, an energy leak is when the horse falls out through one of his shoulders – if we stop the leak by changing his shoulder balance, the energy stays more central and usable. We could also say an energy leak is when he's not responsive enough to the 'go' signal; the energy is leaking out of the back. Or perhaps he is pulling like a train and isn't responsive to the 'stop' signal, in which case the energy would be leaking out of the front!

Lateral balance and straightness

You can work on plugging energy leaks at the front and back of your horse by improving the 'stop' and 'go' responses as discussed in Chapter 7. What about leaking laterally though? In this chapter, I want to talk about side-to-side balance. I like to visualise a ball of energy like a tenpin bowling ball that rolls around inside the horse's body. When the horse has a natural left bend through the neck and loads his right lateral pair of legs, he'll probably be leaking energy (falling through) the right shoulder. Therefore the bowling ball would have rolled towards this area. In order to improve the horse's flexibility and balance, we need to organise matters so that the horse develops capacity to bend his neck easily to the right, and also to develop his loading capacity on the opposite pair of legs; this would entail the ball rolling towards his left shoulder. If we consider this shifting of weight and balance to be key in improving the horse's athletic capabilities with us on board, we can use the distribution of our own weight to influence where the bowling ball rolls and to stabilise it where necessary.

We'll look at the aids for straightness, bending and turning in walk, although they are the same in trot and canter. Often, I find riders don't spend enough time in walk and do not appreciate the value of working on establishing the horse's desired responses in this gait. If you can explain to your horse a 'language of aids' in the walk, he will be able to recognise that same language (albeit perhaps with a lesser degree of precision and balance at first) in trot and canter.

When you work on riding your horse on straight lines, aim to have him completely straight from nose to tail. Owing to the horse's natural asymmetry through the spine, he will need some degree of suppleness already to counter-act this natural tendency to move with a slight curve through the spine. We have

Developing precise control of the shoulders helps with straightness in simple movements and up to complex exercises, like series of flying changes. In this picture the right side of my pelvis has moved through correctly with the flying change, however, my upper body has followed suit a little too much.

already discussed how he will tend to bear most of his weight on one lateral pair (whether right, or left) of legs and therefore his balance point will be towards this side. To walk straight, you need to be aware of this. If he's carrying himself completely straight, your hands should be a totally equal distance either side of his withers, with an absolutely even amount of weight (i.e. not much!) in both reins. So, as you walk on, notice whether or not this is the case. Notice if you feel the need to keep using one leg to push him over to the side. Notice if his neck curves one way; to the left, for instance. If so, your bowling ball of energy will be rolling towards his right shoulder. As his ribcage swings more to the right than the left, this will tend to lift your right hip more than your left, and drop your left hip more than your right. However, depending on your own intrinsic biomechanics, it could also potentially push you over to the right, which would then also be giving your horse a weight aid right. Since he is already falling a bit to the right, that would not be helpful. (Reverse all this if he seems slightly bent to the right!)

In order to centralise his body and bowling ball of energy, first take your attention to the slight dropping of each of your hips, one side and then the other, as the horse walks. Can you feel that one side is dropping more than the other? If so, without 'shoving' with your seat or pushing heavily into the horse, encourage each of your hips to drop exactly the same amount, and notice if you feel a difference in the horse's balance. This can slightly alter the movement in his thoraco-lumbar spine and, through equalising the swing of the ribcage, centralise his weight over his legs to a degree.

Also, whenever you want the horse to make a change of balance through his shoulders, experiment with using a combined aid of shoulder placement, and altering your own balance point. If, for example, you want the horse to shift weight more towards his left shoulder, move your hands as a pair towards the left, without pulling back at all. Bring the right rein towards his neck and the left rein away from it, keeping the reins a parallel distance apart. At the same time, *fractionally* take your weight down into your left thigh (feel as though your thigh is drawing down towards the surface of the school) to give him a weight aid left. He should reorganise his body by moving his shoulders into the space created by your opening left rein and away from the closing right rein, and move under your weight to keep you central on his back. You'll have stopped the energy leaking through the right shoulder and, by moving his shoulders more to the left, you will have successfully rolled his bowling ball more into the middle of his chest. This also helps his hind legs to work with more equal force, and you'll find that bending to the right feels easier too. When you've felt him make the shift, you can bring your hands back to a neutral position and also sit completely equally weighted on your seat bones. As soon as you feel the horse starting to deviate away from this new balance, reapply your aids and straighten him again, remembering to cease those aids when he responds correctly in order to give him the opportunity to move in self-carriage. You shouldn't really need your legs for this; at this stage, we want to save your legs to simply mean 'go', not lots of other things as well.

Above: Walking straight with the balance point central.

Right: Moving the hands sideways to move the balance point to the left.

To recap; if you want the horse to move his shoulders to the left, move both reins to the left and give a tiny weight aid left. If you want him to move his shoulders to the right, move both reins to the right and give a tiny weight aid right. Experiment with doing just that on various lines, to see how he responds, and you will soon get a sense of when his balance in really central. Then try riding on very straight lines and see how much he tries to wobble; avoid trying to micro-manage him to hold him straight through keeping lots of aids clamped on, but see if you can progressively develop self-carriage in his straightness by giving him corrections when he loses balance but leaving him alone when it is good.

Adding bend

Once you have asked the horse to move off as straight as you currently can, you can ask for bend. We are aiming for him to be able to bend, without turning, and to maintain his current line of travel on this straight line. We've already talked about using the bit on the corners of your horse's lips in an upward direction, so this is how you will ask for the bend. He should have an idea of how to move in this way because of the short-rein work you will have already practised in hand. Turn your wrist of the inside hand so your fingers face upwards towards the sky, and then vibrate the rein directly upwards a few inches; the motion comes from a hinging action at your elbow, a little bit like doing a miniature biceps curl, except without a weight! Then lower your hand back to the neutral position. If your horse hasn't offered bend, repeat this action a few times in fairly quick succession – after you've done three or four, your horse should be offering to bend his neck on a light contact.

We still want that invisible glass of liquor on the top of his poll, so if he tries to lean on the bit or drop his neck, lift it back up again to the point you started at. If he brings his head higher, asking for a greater degree of bend should help him come back down to the starting point. You'll need to maintain a soft contact on the outside rein – this is very important. Do not have more contact on the inside than the outside rein. The purpose of the bending is to improve flexibility whilst controlling shoulder balance, but also to develop a connection into the outside rein, so don't give it away! As the horse bends to the inside, he lengthens his neck on the outside and increases the contact on the outside rein. At first, we can allow the outside rein forward a little to enable the horse to bend around. Too tight a contact here would prevent this, but too loose allows him to 'leak' out of his shoulder. However, later on in your training session, keeping your fingers more closed around the outside rein and not yielding it forward will, in fact, cause the horse to come rounder in his outline when you request bend. (*No pulling back though!*)

Turn the wrist and vibrate upwards to ask for inside bend.

Turning

When you are happy that your horse can proceed for some clear strides bending his neck but still walking correctly, ask for him to make a turn. Be very clear in your turning aids, by moving your hands sideways in the direction that you want to go (you can use a very wide opening inside rein at first to encourage the horse to give the correct response) and *also* turning your hips to the inside. Imagine your pelvis is like a steering wheel with power steering! In fact the aim is to turn the hips and upper body as a unit, as if your whole trunk was set in a plaster cast. This provides an efficient turning aid and helps to differentiate from other movements later on. Ensure that you control your horse's shoulder on the circle and be specific where you wish the line to be – disallow him from making the circle bigger or smaller than you intend, by using your sideways reins to move his shoulders left or right as necessary.

Sally is turning her seat and moving her hands to the right to ask the horse to begin the circle.

After you have completed a small circle (10–15m) in good bend, stay on the circle and slowly lengthen your reins to ask your horse to extend his neck and stretch into the contact. The bending encourages him to stretch; he has already had to reach into the outside rein to quite a marked degree anyway, so to reach into the inside one as well is not too difficult. If you ask for him to extend his neck and stretch after you have done quite a bit of bending work on both reins, it will probably work even better as he will already have lengthened both sides of his neck.

Change the rein frequently in walk and see if you can establish straightness, then bend, then turn. Also ask him frequently to extend his neck and stretch, and then bring him back up again to play with his balance point.

When you are both confident in walk, try the same process in trot and then canter on both reins. Even if your horse is already working at a high level, use these exercises in your warm-up and you will find that they deliver more suppleness and expression in your work.

Preparing the ingredients

When you ride any movement in the school, try to set up the 'ingredients' you need before you actually ask for the movement. For instance, if you are planning to turn onto a 10m circle, ask for bend at least three or four metres beforehand – when training, if the horse doesn't release to the bend properly, don't ask or permit him to make the turn onto the circle until he has done so. For every corner that you ride, ask for the bend beforehand and then specifically ask for the turn – don't just rely on the fact that he follows the track, or you are going to find yourself in trouble when it comes to riding in an area where there is no fence or track to stick to.

You can also ask the horse to make turns without setting up any bend at all beforehand, so he has to keep very straight and really mobilise his shoulders. You will do this in the same way as asking for the turn, just from a totally straight line instead of asking for bend first. Doing this type of turn on squares or diamond shapes is very useful to emphasise the 'turn' response and to work on precise shoulder control.

Dealing with incorrect responses

What if it doesn't work? Your horse might not respond to the reins moving sideways, so what do you do now? You can only bring one rein into his neck to a certain point before it might cross over his withers, which we don't want. So, if he doesn't respond, you can try moving your pair of reins with repeated sideways actions, rather than one constant pressure, which he could block against. Do this quite firmly in a rhythmic motion, taking care not to cross the outside rein over his neck. The other thing to try is opening the inside rein much further away from his neck – this will mean that the reins are no longer parallel, but that is fine. As long as your horse can feel the outside rein closing against his neck it can help him a lot to feel the inside one really opening to make it very clear. If that still doesn't help, tap the whip near or on his shoulder as in the groundwork exercises. You will need to use these increased pressures in order to motivate the response you want quickly (remember the 3-second rule?) in order to make the lesson clear to your horse.

Combining the signals

These logical signals then combine to create other movements. For example, we can look at Sally and Lottie, who we met earlier. Sally plans to ride a shoulder-in whilst on the left rein. Before Sally comes to a corner, she sets up left bend. After turning Lottie through the corner, she asks her to turn her shoulders to the inside for yet another step. As soon as Lottie takes that step, Sally changes her balance point to give a weight aid to the outside and also moves her hands a little to the outside to stop the turn from continuing, and instead facilitates the movement to the right down the track as she touches Lottie with her inside (left) leg. She might have to touch her on the hip with her whip as well to keep the quarters on the track. As a result of breaking the movement down into simple steps and checking that these are easily achieved before adding the next stage, she achieves her goal – shoulder-in.

Simple signals can combine to create other movements such as shoulder-in.

Practising off the horse

You can practise the aids described above in combination with balancing on a Swiss ball; perhaps also your sitting trot simulation by wrapping your stretch band around something sturdy and then use your bounce-and-push-the-button exercise. Can you maintain a really light feel on the elastic? Do you find yourself pulling on it as you try to balance? Practise doing your Swiss ball series along with your stretch band sometimes to help you develop an independent feel on the reins as you move.

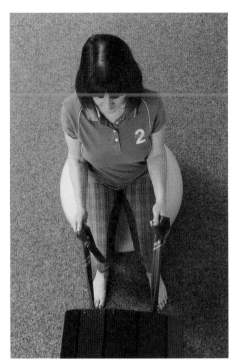 

Holding your stretch band like a pair of reins gives you feedback of how your balance might affect your contact with the horse's mouth.

Practising your Swiss ball exercises combined with the rein aids to bend and turn helps to train those movement patterns in your body.

CHAPTER ELEVEN

Mind Matters – the Mind/Body Connection

Jane Reid.

'm delighted to include this fascinating chapter which, apart from this introductory paragraph, was written by my mother, Jane Reid, who is a clinical hypnotherapist and EFT practitioner. She discovered the potency of these techniques after a serious bolting accident caused her early retirement from her career as a head teacher in 1996. She has a wealth of experience in helping riders, including myself, and we work closely together. All the biomechanical and technical coaching in the world can be of limited value if there is an emotional blockage or if the fear response is present, both of which are extremely detrimental to physical performance.

You may be wondering why on earth you've come upon this particular chapter in a book you've bought to learn more about core connection. Well, the approach for both horse and rider at The Dressage Studio is a holistic one, so, for us, considering the role of the mind is absolutely essential.

The mind and the body

It's interesting that some people assume that the mind/body connection is either spiritual, intangible or metaphorical, but it is, in fact, an entire branch of science. The most prominent of these is known as psycho-neuro-immunology which is the effect of the mind on health and the resistance to disease.

The idea that a mind/body connection actually exists has been a fundamental part of Eastern medicine for centuries, but it is only more recently that Western medicine has started to consider exactly how – through which mechanisms – the mind and body communicate. It has been found that part of the brain called the hypothalamic-limbic system acts as a central computer for all systems of the body. It takes the language of the higher brain (your thoughts) and translates them into the 'language' of your body (your messenger molecules). These messenger molecules travel to the system they're communicating with and let the cells know how to function.

The brain is in constant communication with each system of the body. For our purposes here, you should be aware that, when you are riding (and at any time at all), your thoughts are definitely translated into chemical messages that your body receives and the route they take is known as a neural pathway.

The conscious and the subconscious

When considering mind matters it is interesting to be aware of the difference between the conscious and subconscious. The conscious mind, which is responsible for managing our verbal language, maths, decisions and logic, is actually a very small part of the human brain (only 10%) and it is very heavily influenced by the other 90% – the subconscious mind. As well as being responsible for your autonomic nervous system, heart rate and temperature control, the subconscious stores all your memories (even if you thought they were long forgotten) and is responsible for your habits, emotions and processing all your experiences. It actually processes 2 million pieces of information every single second, only passing on a handful of the most important to the conscious mind and disregarding the rest. In contrast, our conscious mind is only able to hold about seven things in the short-term memory at any one time. Maybe you've found yourself multi-tasking and becoming stressed and forgetful and this is because, when you're trying to think about several things at once and those seven-ish spaces are already taken, it's extremely easy to forget where your car keys are or forget part of a dressage test or whatever it is you're trying to concentrate on which is that one item too many.

Our subconscious mind does its very best to help keep space free in our conscious minds for those seven(ish) items. How does it do this? Well, we only have to repeat new things a few times and they quickly become learned behaviour – something we don't have to think about at all. When we have established sufficient neural pathways our behaviour becomes automatic because it is inefficient to take up thinking space in our conscious mind. I wonder if you can remember how, when learning to tie your shoelaces, you struggled initially? And what about when you learned to drive? Did it demand all your concentration to co-ordinate the accelerator and clutch with everything else a driver has to do? Maybe you thought you would never, ever master it and yet here you are driving without much of a thought – unconsciously.

This help from our subconscious mind, to take learning on in this way, is amazingly useful when we create automatic behaviour or habits that we want and are helpful, but the huge downside is that we also create as a habit anything that we repeat. Our subconscious is unable to differentiate between required and not required and so it merely takes on any repeated behaviour as automatic. Try to bear this in mind from time to time. Something like your daily mucking out is probably always done from the same side, and it would no doubt feel very strange indeed if you tried using your fork differently. Similarly, the way you sit at a computer and also drive, not to forget the way you sit on a horse, is locked into your subconscious mind for you so that you don't have to 'think'.

Changing subconscious behaviour

The good news is that all those neural pathways you've laid down though constant repetition need not be permanent. If you have some behaviour or habit that you would like to change it is a case of breaking the cycle to enable these neural pathways to reduce and eventually disappear. Fortunately we are perfectly able to create new ones, but at first it really will require some effort.

To break any learned habit, whether it's smoking, overeating or the asymmetric position we adopt on a horse, there is a 'recipe' for breaking it, which consists of six steps:

1. *You need to become consistently aware of what is happening.* Without being aware, nothing will change and just being aware every so often won't bring about lasting change.

2. *You need to find some way to break the pattern of the habit.* When your brain is ingrained into one particular response it will need a jolt to come out of its groove. So, choose something different, however small, to do instead, e.g. instead of having a cigarette take a walk around the garden or do some EFT tapping (you'll learn exactly how to do this later in this chapter). When you first get on your horse allow yourself to become completely relaxed, almost like a rag doll.

3. *You must now choose what you want instead!* Again, think of a smoker; most people give up smoking and take up ... well, eating chocolate éclairs or biting their nails! The thing is, if you don't consciously choose what you want instead,

your brain will most certainly find something – and it may not be all that helpful for you!

4. *You have to implement the new choice.* It's no use just thinking about it – you actually have to do it!

5. *You need reward.* Pavlov was right, you know…. Not only are we creatures of habit, but we are very similar to puppies in that we appreciate a pat on the back and a little treat – we always move towards pleasure and away from pain. So make the effort of change worth your while and give yourself good feedback. This can be as simple as saying a big 'Well done' to yourself.

6. *You have to repeat* – it's like building muscles; if you lift weights only once it won't change a thing. It's repetition that makes the difference! You are creating new neural pathways and eventually the new behaviour will become automatic.

When you're in the process of unlearning and replacing old habits or patterns with new ones, I'd like to suggest that you harness the power of your mind to help you whenever you can, as it's a mighty powerful tool!

You can do this in several ways, but first I would urge you to make use of your imagination and I can't emphasise this enough. Imagination can help us in an amazing way and be your best friend, but it's probably the case that it may have been more of a worst enemy for a lot of riders. If this is the case for you, you can turn it around by following the six steps above.

Proper use of our imagination is so effective because our subconscious mind is actually unable to tell the difference between what is really happening and what we're imagining – whatever thoughts or images are present in our imagination at any one time are absolutely 'real'. Have a think for a moment about your own inner voice when you're riding, or about to compete. What images do you sometimes have in your mind when your self-talk is wondering whether your horse might bolt, rear, buck, crash through that jump or spook violently at the flowers at C? Your body can respond as though these things are reality, can't it! If you've experienced this you'll know just how powerfully your imagination can affect you – but not for the good, that's for sure. So, what about breaking this cycle? What about unlearning this and laying down neural pathways for patterns and behaviour conducive to confidence and harmony?

'Is this really possible?', I hear you say. 'How on earth can I use my imagination to stop these scary feelings?' The answer is that yes, it is very definitely possible and to do it you need to acquire the skills of mental rehearsal and visualisation, which are fantastic tools for any rider – or indeed anyone.

Mental rehearsal

In his book *The Winning Mind*, British Olympic javelin thrower Steve Backley tells of the time he sprained his ankle just four weeks before the competition season. He was immobile for two weeks and throughout this time concentrated on detailed mental rehearsal. Mentally, he threw his javelin in every stadium where he would be competing. In real time he imagined the minutiae of fluent, perfect throws and at the end of his enforced break he was able to carry on with his training exactly where he had left off.

The neural pathways I have mentioned can be stimulated and even *created* in imagination, which is food for thought, indeed.

There has been a lot written about the power of mental training but for our purposes I'll just mention a couple of things. When I was at a CDP (Continued Professional Development) course at a London clinic some time ago, our attention was drawn to research carried out by Russians when they compared four groups of Olympic athletes in terms of their training schedules. The first group undertook 100% physical training, the second 75% physical and 25% mental, the third did 50% of each and the fourth undertook 25% physical and 75% mental training. Which group performed the best do you think? Well my guess was Group 3 but in fact it was Group 4!

When I was in my twenties and thirties I tried my hand at golf and my hero at that time was Jack Nicklaus. If only I'd known about his mental approach then I might have improved more! I've since learned that he never, ever hit a shot – not even a practice shot – without first looking at exactly where he wanted the ball to land and then visualising a detailed movie with the perfect backswing and follow through to achieve his purpose.

Never underestimate the power of detailed mental rehearsal whatever your riding discipline or sport – or even for things like job interviews.

To use mental rehearsal effectively you need to be able involve as many of your senses as possible. Some of us find that visualising is easy for us, some of us are more auditory (concerned with hearing), and some of us more kinaesthetic (concerned with touching/doing) but we must try to involve all these – even smells and tastes if we possibly can. The following two exercises will help you to identify (if you don't already know) which of the senses you find easy to use and which are more difficult and once you're aware of this you'll be able to make an extra effort with the weak ones when you start using mental rehearsal properly.

▶ Exercise 1

If you can ask someone to read this out to you very slowly, all the better.

Imagine you're in your kitchen.… On one of the worktops is a basket of lemons … I'd like you to reach out and choose one of the ripe, shiny yellow lemons. Notice the weight of the lemon in your hand … and also notice how it feels as you slide your fingers over the smooth, waxy skin. What does the dimpled texture feel like? I want you to lift the lemon to your face now … and breathe in that lemony smell.… Now slice the lemon open and notice what the bright, yellow flesh looks like as you see the juice running out. Bite down on it … and be aware of the juice running over your tongue … and your mouth fills with the taste of lemon juice.

Was it easy for you to see as well as smell and taste, I wonder?

▶ Exercise 2

Think about a meal that you may be going to have tomorrow. Allow yourself a few moments so that you have as clear a picture of it as possible in your mind. What exactly will that meal look, taste and smell like? How will it feel in your mouth? Imagine your favourite tune is playing in the background as you eat. Imagine the food is in front of you now and you can really smell the aromas. Bring a portion towards your mouth and notice how much stronger the aroma is now. Savour that aroma for a moment and look carefully at the food. What colours do you see? Are they vivid or dull? Is the food in sharp focus or a bit fuzzy? Now pop it into your mouth and be aware of the textures and temperature. Chew slowly and

188 • CORE CONNECTION FOR RIDER AND HORSE

allow your taste buds a full experience. Can you taste it? Are you salivating even though this is imaginary food? What about the music; can you hear it? Is it a CD or radio? What is it playing? Is it loud or soft? Can you turn the volume up in your head and then turn it down again? Can you speed it up and then slow it down?

How easy was this exercise for you I wonder? We often favour one sense more than the others and there is often one (or more) that we find difficult. Which was your clearest and which do you need to work on?

Now that you're aware which sense (or perhaps more than one) is more difficult for you to involve, you can try to make some improvement. For instance, if hearing the radio music in the exercise wasn't easy for you, concentrate on what sounds you can hear as you are out and about or just sitting relaxing somewhere. A bit later on, when you're somewhere else, close your eyes and try to replay the same sounds to yourself. You may have to begin with one or two sounds and then gradually increase them. You'll notice if you do this that being aware of sounds in mental rehearsal becomes easier.

As mentioned, in mental rehearsal using as many senses as possible is important. Let's say you want to visualise yourself on your horse; you need to do this in minute detail for it to be properly effective. First, see the perfect picture, the one you want to create as though you are looking at a movie. To help you, actually hear the words that the person who assists you with your position always says; words like lengthen, lift, open, heavy or soft – those words that are particular to you. Watch the movie as your body changes slightly on hearing these cues. Maybe your trainer gives touch cues sometimes and will touch your lower back, your stomach, or in between your shoulders to help you to adjust your position. If so, actually feel them in your visualisation and again watch the movie to observe any changes.

Now it's time to put yourself in the movie, so that you're no longer seeing it from the outside but are actually starring in it. Merge yourself into your body in the picture and actually feel the horse underneath you. Be aware of your feet in the stirrups and the exact sensation of your saddle, and the reins in your fingers. If this isn't easy for you just relax, take a few deep breaths and imagine this all once again.

This is only the start, of course, but if you can do this well, you have the basics. I wonder what smells you're aware of; maybe leather or the tack cleaner you use, or fly spray; maybe just that lovely horse breath or the hay that the farmer next door is making right now? Whatever it is, notice it.

Now you're ready to mentally rehearse your test, or jumping course, or whatever it is you wish to do. Remember to be in the movie; don't see yourself from afar. Feel your horse's every stride. If you're mentally rehearsing a dressage test do it in real time so that a test lasting 4½ minutes will take you exactly the same amount of time to visualise. Always ride exactly as you want it to be on the day – your perfect test. Sometimes it helps to pretend you're someone else when you do this – someone you admire – especially if you're lacking confidence. As you get more and more used to doing this, you can begin to feel your horse putting in a spook (or whatever he tends to do) and always deal with it perfectly, just continuing really well with the next movement – riding in the moment, aware of the feelings, sounds, etc. If you don't like people watching you, just see the face of your best friend or your trainer on every strange face; see a smile and hear what they'd be saying to you.

When you finish the test imagine in a lot of detail coming out and being met with 'Well dones' from people. See their faces, hear their exact words, hear what you're saying to your horse and feel his neck as you stroke and pat him. Feel how thrilled you are!

All this creates neural pathways so that when you get to your test for real your body and mind have a start; you've 'been' there before and know what to do.

Some clients ask me how often they should do this and I'd say at least once a day for several days before you compete, jump your course, hack or whatever it is you're mentally rehearsing.

You may perhaps wonder how you can mentally rehearse a hack. Many riders would never need to do so, but for others hacking presents fear of what they're likely to pass or meet. Involving all the senses you can, as above, see your perfect hack; see a movie of you riding an effective shoulder-in past something that bothers you, or see a movie of you using your practised stopping technique perfectly if your horse has taken fright. Always see yourself in control. Importantly, then merge yourself into the picture so that you are actually riding, and then repeat. Remember to feel the horse underneath you, the stirrups and reins; ride every single stride in real time. Hear a friend praising you afterwards – use your imagination and play with this as it will reap rich rewards.

Do your beliefs affect your riding?

What we believe affects everything we do, including our riding. I don't mean spiritual beliefs but those things we 'know' to be true.

The power of beliefs

Years ago I read about a man who had been found dead in one of those huge refrigeration units and the autopsy showed that his body had frozen to death. The strange thing was though, that there had been no power connected to the unit and the temperature in there was well above freezing. How could his body have frozen? It could only be deduced that because he knew where he was and believed ('knew') that he was going to freeze to death, over time that is what happened.

Many of us have heard, too, of people who have recovered from life-threatening illnesses because they have a particular mental attitude and believe ('know') that they will get well.

What we believe is more important than we may realise in all areas of life and I'd like to mention Roger Bannister here who, you'll remember, was the first person to run the 4-minute mile in the 1950s. No one even dreamed that this could be achieved, but Bannister was a medical student and earnestly believed that physiologically there was no reason to prevent the human body achieving this. Coupled with his belief ('knowing'), he put in an enormous amount of physical training, together with vivid mental rehearsal involving himself in the race. He was successful, of course, but the interesting thing for me is that the following year thirty-nine other people achieved this too, and the year after that over a hundred more people did it. Now, even college students achieve the 4-minute mile and it isn't just because running shoes have improved dramatically in sixty years; they just 'know' (believe) that it's possible to achieve.

And while considering the importance of beliefs I should mention that the world's most researched drug is the placebo, which is shown to be amazingly effective. Apparently the bigger the pill, the more effective it is – and injections are more powerful still!

I recently watched a Derren Brown programme on television concerning the placebo effect. He chose an unsuspecting group of people who suffered badly from fear; one was very afraid of heights, one wanted to be a solo singer but her fear was preventing her even though she was very talented, and another suffered from a crippling social phobia and was too shy to speak to anyone he didn't know. Brown had set up a wonderfully realistic, lavishly kitted out fake research centre and laboratory complete with 'doctors' and he took the group there to show them around. It was important to go to every length to ensure that the group totally believed in what they were being shown. This was the home of a drug called Remmydin (as far as I recall) which had been developed there by scientists to remove the physical symptoms of fear and it was explained that it had been trialled on soldiers in combat with great effect. Now the researchers wanted to trial it more widely and the group was asked if they would like to experience the drug and feed back their experiences. It all seemed extremely realistic; they were even taken to see a man in a lab setting who had taken the drug and was now being administered an electric shock every few minutes. They were asked to observe his heart rate monitor which showed absolutely no anticipation whatsoever of the shock to come. Amazing! (In fact the heart monitor was attached to the 'doctor' in the room – just an added touch in order to make the drug utterly and completely credible.)

The volunteers were all desperate to trial the drug because they were all so crippled by their fears, and the injections were duly administered. The effect was remarkably quick on the young man with the fear of heights. After previously being too afraid to walk across a normal road bridge, by the end of the programme he was confidently standing right at the edge of somewhere very frighteningly high up. The man who had been afraid to engage in conversation was now capable of happily engaging in market research in the street and even stepped in to stop a brawl in a pub. The girl who wanted to sing had successfully attended an audition but it had taken her much longer to achieve confidence and Brown had to assist her with some hypnosis. These people were amazed to eventually discover that this drug didn't exist and that it had been just the power of their own minds which had given them permission to have a go and to be successful. Remmydin is, in fact, an anagram of Re my mind!

What we believe then is paramount, because our belief systems drive the way we think, feel and behave. Many of us have limiting beliefs which can have an incredibly negative or damaging effect on our lives. A limiting belief is any thought or belief that doesn't help us to achieve the life we really want. I wonder what yours are? Here are some examples: I'm not very clever, I expect failure to happen, I'm not good enough, I don't deserve (to do well, to own this lovely horse, etc.). If you have a limited belief it can detrimentally affect all aspects of your life – how you respond at school, your career choice, how you function in a relationship and so on.

Many of our basic beliefs are created when, as children, we pick things up from our parents, teachers and other adults. Maybe you can even hear the voice of someone telling you something when you were small which helped to form a belief about yourself that you still have today. It may be that your adults caused a lack of confidence and self-esteem, or in some way held you back from reaching your potential – but if you were lucky, your adults taught you from being little what a great and unique person you are and that you deserve to reach for the stars.

Changing beliefs

Beliefs can change of course, which is good as we don't want to take outdated beliefs from others into adulthood since they can become millstones. Some change naturally over years: we all probably believed in Santa Claus and the tooth fairy at one point, but over time these particular beliefs have been replaced.

We can change limiting beliefs with some effort and first it can be helpful to recognise where a belief originated. If it was from a parent or teacher we need to acknowledge that they probably had our well-being at heart and were doing the best they knew, but now we're grown up we can choose to leave this behind if that's what we want. We can then begin looking for evidence so that we can begin to believe something new. If you've been feeling that you're not good enough, for instance, really look for those times when you definitely are. It's likely that you have just not noticed them previously owing to something called confirmation bias; this means that you are far more likely to see events and experiences that confirm your belief system rather than ones that challenge it.

So it's really important to work on changing the 'I'll never achieve' beliefs such as, 'I can't jump more than three feet' or 'I'll never get a proper half-pass'. You can begin by saying the opposite out aloud to begin with and visualise yourself doing it really well – put your heart and soul into it just as we practised earlier. You'll soon notice some difference!

We can work on beliefs we want to change with Emotional Freedom Technique (EFT) and the results can be amazingly liberating. I'll be explaining how to use EFT as a self-help tool for riding-related anxieties a little further on.

Our minds and the stress response

If you are a nervous rider or competitor you're likely to know all about the stress response! It is a primal instinct, of course, which has ensured the very survival of our species, so let's now remind ourselves just now how it functioned for early man.

Let me introduce our caveman. We'll call him Bob. Let's imagine he is taking a walk looking for food when suddenly a great big sabre-toothed tiger jumps out in front of him with a glint in its eye and rather hungry. Bob now has three options: he's either going to fight the sabre-toothed tiger, or maybe run for his life, or perhaps he'll freeze on the spot and hope he hasn't been spotted. Whichever Bob chooses there's no doubt that he'll need every scrap of available energy to deal with the situation and it's at this moment that the sympathetic nervous system activates. This is the part of the autonomic nervous system responsible for the fight, flight response, or stress response.

What exactly happens to Bob when the sympathetic nervous system activates? Well, his breathing becomes shallow in order to speed up oxygen supplies to his main muscles. His heart rate and blood pressure increase to rush blood to his arms and legs and, since there's no point in concern for that graze on his knee from earlier, since he may well be dead in a few seconds, any healing stops as Bob's immune system shuts down. The stress hormones adrenalin and cortisol flood his bloodstream to overcome any fatigue, as that's the very last thing he needs at the moment. Suddenly, digesting the woolly mammoth he ate for lunch is much less of a physiological priority and he experiences 'butterflies' in his stomach. He may well even soil himself or vomit in order to free up all available energy in his body, because digesting food uses a considerable amount of energy – more than working out at the gym for an hour. Blood can now be directed away from his internal organs to his muscles and brain. Bob's saliva will dry up as the glands take a rest and all his senses become increasingly alert. Also his blood-clotting mechanisms are activated to allow him to burn more energy and his muscles become tense and ready for action.

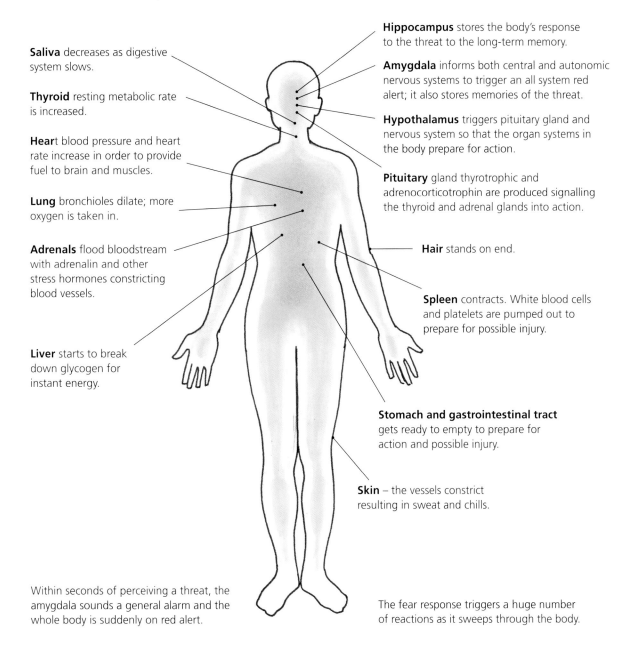

Saliva decreases as digestive system slows.

Thyroid resting metabolic rate is increased.

Heart blood pressure and heart rate increase in order to provide fuel to brain and muscles.

Lung bronchioles dilate; more oxygen is taken in.

Adrenals flood bloodstream with adrenalin and other stress hormones constricting blood vessels.

Liver starts to break down glycogen for instant energy.

Hippocampus stores the body's response to the threat to the long-term memory.

Amygdala informs both central and autonomic nervous systems to trigger an all system red alert; it also stores memories of the threat.

Hypothalamus triggers pituitary gland and nervous system so that the organ systems in the body prepare for action.

Pituitary gland thyrotrophic and adrenocorticotrophin are produced signalling the thyroid and adrenal glands into action.

Hair stands on end.

Spleen contracts. White blood cells and platelets are pumped out to prepare for possible injury.

Stomach and gastrointestinal tract gets ready to empty to prepare for action and possible injury.

Skin – the vessels constrict resulting in sweat and chills.

Within seconds of perceiving a threat, the amygdala sounds a general alarm and the whole body is suddenly on red alert.

The fear response triggers a huge number of reactions as it sweeps through the body.

Do any of these fight/flight symptoms ring a bell with you – even though you've most probably never encountered a sabre-toothed tiger?

The great news for Bob is that, if he survives, within a very short period of time the threat is over and he can go back to his own business. To enable him to do this, his parasympathetic nervous system activates and endorphins are released to bring his body back to homeostastis, or balance.

Physiologically, the human species hasn't changed much for thousands of years and the fight/flight response for us today is identical to our friend Bob's. The thing is, though, that our environment has changed beyond all recognition! Whilst such a response is crucial in a life-and-death crisis it is totally inappropriate for the majority of our present-day stress triggers. I like to compare it with a faulty airbag in a car. An airbag is the perfect thing to have in an emergency when it inflates to protect us from injuries, but an overactive bag that inflates every time we touch the brake would most certainly prevent us from driving safely. Similarly, the fight/flight response isn't wholly appropriate for when we're just running late for an important meeting, or the internet is down; these modern-day stressors occur too frequently and the continuation of our lives does not depend on them!

A huge thing to consider also is the fact that the fight/flight or stress response is triggered whether a danger is real or *merely perceived* – remember what I said earlier about our subconscious mind not being able to differentiate between what's real and what's imagined? Indeed, just your thoughts alone can activate a whole host of physical symptoms as experienced by Bob, so whenever you're thinking negatively about that job interview or worrying about a relationship, the stress symptoms will manifest themselves.

Performance anxiety

And this brings us appropriately to performance anxiety. As some of you may have experienced, merely thinking about entering the competition arena can cause us to want to go to the loo, to sweat, to make our heart beat faster and our muscles tense, etc. Trying to ride a dressage test or jump a course with our bodies thus affected is certainly not easy, especially as underneath us we have a very sensitive half-ton prey animal! Feeling all that tension above, we can hardly blame him for wondering where on earth the imminent danger is and for behaving accordingly, can we?

So we need to break the cycle. When the rider becomes calm and relaxed the horse is very much more likely to follow suit. To this end, the time you put in beforehand on mental rehearsal, as described earlier, will reap a very rich reward. Another hugely powerful tool is the use of Emotional Freedom Technique.

Emotional Freedom Technique (EFT)

EFT may well be new to you and, like me when I was first introduced to it, you may be extremely sceptical. After all, we are intelligent people! I would say read on and just go with it because, although it sounds quite wacky, it works!

EFT (sometimes called tapping) has been likened to acupuncture without the needles and I actually like to think of it a 'psychological acupuncture'. The tapping techniques are a series of astoundingly fast and easy processes that anyone can learn, leading to genuine freedom from negative emotion.

The principle of EFT is that the cause of all negative emotion is a disruption in the body's energy system. When you use the technique, you focus on your problem whilst tapping on various meridian points on your face and body and, as you do so, a cognitive shift takes place enabling you to think differently. This appears to occur as an energy disturbance related to your problem is released. It is an amazingly successful technique for phobias, anxiety, stress, self-esteem issues and healing trauma and it has been described as one of the most important breakthroughs of the twentieth century in the area of psychology.

The principles of EFT were discovered by Dr Roger Callahan, an American clinical psychologist of over forty years experience and an acupuncturist with an interest in Eastern medicine. He had made it his life's work to find ways to cure people of unfounded fears, phobias and anxieties. He finally came across some techniques that proved to be extremely successful and there is a much-told story of his client, Mary, who had suffered from a severe water phobia for many years. She was unable to look at large volumes of water and she even found having a bath in two inches of water extremely traumatic. Dr Callahan had used all his skills including non-standard treatments such as hypnosis with little improvement. Then, on one occasion, Mary mentioned to him that the sight of water made her feel sick and at that point Dr Callahan asked her to tap underneath her eye, which is an important acupuncture, acupressure and stomach meridian point. Mary immediately felt free of her phobia and ran out to dangle her legs in his pool. She was instantaneously cured and all these many years later, her phobia has not returned.

Dr Callahan then spent a long time refining and researching his method, which became known as 'Thought Field Therapy' on the grounds that thoughts related to the energy field in the body and that changing this energy field by tapping on the meridian points could release negative emotions happily and easily. Treatments are based on algorithms or particular sequences of tapping points to relieve specific problems and TFT gained widespread acceptance.

Over time, Gary Craig developed Emotional Freedom Technique from Dr Callahan's Thought Field Therapy. He very much wanted to simplify it and he did so by using all the acupressure points for every presenting problem instead of learning all the many algorithms. Whichever point or points were the correct ones, therefore, would always be covered. Gary Craig wanted to provide an effective system that anyone could learn to use very easily and quickly as a self-help tool. He has devoted many years of his life to this end, retiring in 2010.

You can learn about EFT and how to apply it in much more detail than this brief chapter allows at Gary Craig's website www.emofree.com. I am continually amazed, as a practitioner, how it allows riders to let go of both rational and irrational fears regarding past accidents and 'what ifs'. From the information in this chapter you'll be able to use EFT at a basic self-help level, which can be extremely empowering. The instantaneous changes like Mary's do happen on occasions, but this is usually when the problem is a phobia like fear of spiders for instance. Be prepared to spend a few minutes two or three times a week on your riding-related fears and worries, and notice the difference! Some of you may prefer to see a practitioner who is trained in advanced techniques and can provide you with results sooner. However, I do encourage you to play with the techniques yourself as great results are possible.

On the diagrams below and opposite you'll see the tapping points on the face, body and hand.

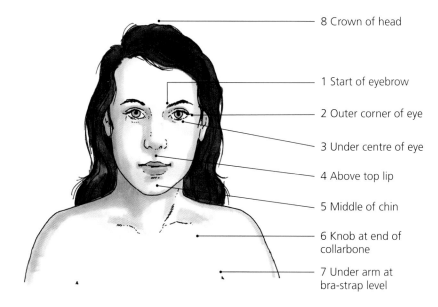

8 Crown of head

1 Start of eyebrow

2 Outer corner of eye

3 Under centre of eye

4 Above top lip

5 Middle of chin

6 Knob at end of collarbone

7 Under arm at bra-strap level

The EFT tapping points.

Without involving any words for now, have a practice at tapping them. Tap using two fingers and about seven times (it doesn't matter exactly how many). Tap so that you can feel it, but not so hard that it hurts! Point number 7 is actually under your arm where we ladies have our bras, and you can use the flat of your hand to tap here. Tap the whole sequence a few times whilst breathing into your diaphragm and not just your upper chest. This is, in itself, a wonderful tool if ever you are feeling anxious or panicky (detailed information on breathing is given in *Pilates for Riders*) because the tapping allows electromagnetic pulses to travel to the amygdala (the part of the brain triggering the flight/fight response) and the production of adrenalin and cortisol is calmed. If you are actually feeling anxious, you can sit and repeat this tapping sequence for several minutes; just breathe deeply and calmly into your diaphragm and allow the tapping to do its work. It is something that you can't really do when in public or riding, of course, but when you are used to feeling the effect of this at home there is an effective shortcut that you can use in this situation that I'll explain later in the chapter.

Now I'd like you to find the 'karate chop' point on your hand as in the diagram. Tap with two fingers on the side of your hand at the place you would use if you were doing a karate chop. Again, tap so that you can feel it and about seven times.

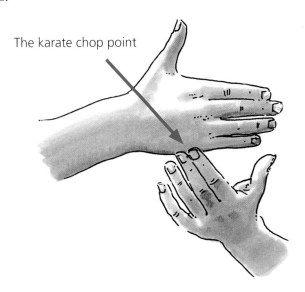

The karate chop point

Learning EFT involves both tapping and words – which we will come on to shortly – but first I'd like you to experiment with the following exercise as for many of you (not all maybe) it will demonstrate how tapping can make a difference. In this case, I'd like you to notice in a breathing exercise any difference in your lung capacity before and after tapping. This is something I often do with groups in workshops and is just for demonstration purposes. After the group has done this, they are usually even keener to learn the next step regarding EFT and their own riding concerns.

First, take a deep breath, right down into your diaphragm. Now do this once more and this time give a score out of ten to the amount of air you feel you've taken into your lungs. Few of us breathe in to full capacity (a 10); give yourself a score which is just for comparison purposes later. I'll score myself a 7.

Now begin to tap your hand on the karate chop point and as, you continue, say out loud (if you are really sceptical please just go with it!) *'Even though I can only breathe in to a 7 (insert your own score here), I truly and deeply accept myself'*.

Repeat this another two times.

Now you are going to tap points 1–8, remembering to tap about seven times on each point. As you tap, I'd like you to repeat a reminder phrase out loud at each point. *'I can breathe to a 7'* (insert your own score).

Repeat the whole tapping sequence and reminder phrase another twice.

Finally, take another deep breath into your diaphragm, slowly exhale and now see if there is any difference to your original score. How much have you been able to fill your lungs this time? For me, the difference is very noticeable and I'll now give a score of 9. In workshops most people find a noticeable difference too, but just occasionally there may be little or no difference. Try the whole process again using your new score (if there is one) and see if your lung capacity can be further improved.

I repeat that the purpose of the above is for demonstration only and to familiarise you with the application of the basic recipe of EFT. If tapping in this way can make a difference to our breathing, it will surely be interesting to see what it can do when we start to apply it as it is meant to be used, on our thoughts, memories and our emotions.

So, before we move on to using EFT to help any riding-related anxieties, let's have a go at tapping on something minor in your every day life that really irks you and see if we can make a difference to your feelings about it. Again, I often ask groups to do this in workshops and, just as here, the reason is twofold: as well as providing interesting results you are becoming more practised at the mechanics of finding the tapping points and applying the basic EFT recipe.

First then, I'd like you to bring to mind something small that thoroughly irritates you; it may be something like your partner or children always leaving wet towels on the bathroom floor, or perhaps those annoying drivers who're always right at your tail. It could even be someone at work who borrows items from your desk. When you have something in mind, give a score out of 10 to how much this bothers you (10 being 100%) – and again, this is just for comparison purposes later when you 'test' to see if the tapping has brought about any change.

We then need to decide on what Gary Craig calls the set-up phrase and in this you'll notice that we are accepting ourselves even with our particular problem. This is an important stage of the process which is to counteract any self-defeating, negative thinking which is outside your awareness and which will hinder the success of EFT (and also any other therapy that you may undertake too). This is the reason why some people have such a difficult time losing weight, for instance, or why very talented athletes can freeze and never reach their true potential. It will be present in many of us occasionally, and in some of us much of the time; even the most positive people are subject to it. As the set-up only takes a few seconds, if it isn't present then no harm's done and a major impediment to your success will be out of the way.

So, let's return to the set-up phrase which will be something like this: *'Even though I feel really angry when Bill leaves his towels on the bathroom floor, I truly and deeply accept myself.'*

Or: *'Even though I panic when people drive on my tail I truly and deeply accept myself.'*

Or: *'Even though I'm really irritated when Jill takes my things I truly and deeply accept myself.'*

I'm sure you get the idea; insert your own words where necessary. If you're really not comfortable saying that you deeply and completely accept yourself, instead you can say something like, *'I'm okay'*.

Say your phrase out loud three times, like we did before, as you tap the karate chop point on your hand continuously.

Then tap points 1–8 on your face and body about seven times and at each point say a reminder phrase. For example:

'Bill leaves his towel'

'People driving on my tail'

'Jill taking my things'

The reason for the reminder phrase is that, at this moment, we're not actually feeling how we would if we'd just come upon Bill's soggy towels so the energy disruption caused by those feelings isn't present. Tuning in and thinking about the issue, together with the repetition of the reminder phrase, is reminding your system of the problem so that the negative energy it causes is present and can therefore be shifted by the tapping. It's the tapping on the meridian points that does the work!

As before, repeat the tapping sequence on points 1–8 with the reminder phrase another twice.

Take a deep breath and exhale slowly, have a little stretch and tune in to whatever problem you were working on. What was your previous score for how much 'Bill's towels' bothered you? What will you score it out of 10 now? Has it decreased? Hopefully it has decreased a little.

It isn't often that one round of tapping will reduce your score to 2 or below and so we go again. The only difference in subsequent rounds it that when we say the set-up phrase, we slightly adjust it for best results. Again, it is to do with any self-sabotage that may be present and which may block any remaining progress. In the first round we have already shifted some of the energy disturbance surrounding our problem, but we want to shift it all if we can. If you want to find out more about this psychological reversal (as it's called) do have a look at Gary Craig's website or read his *EFT Manual*. There are also many other good books available.

So, in subsequent rounds, the adjustment in the set-up phrase is:

'*Even though I still have* some *of this anger about* (Bill leaving his towels) *I deeply and completely accept myself.*'

Or: '*Even though I still have* some *of this anger* (about people driving on my tail) *I deeply and completely accept myself.*'

Or: '*Even though I still have* some *annoyance about* (Jill at work) *I deeply and completely accept myself.*'

As before, tap the karate chop point continuously as you say this three times and also repeat the tapping sequence on points 1–8 three times whilst saying your reminder phrase.

Take a deep breath, exhale slowly, tune in to your problem and score it once again. It may take a few of the subsequent rounds to get to 0, or you may only manage to get to something like a 2 – even so, you'll notice that you now feel differently about what was bothering you.

Once you have learned the tapping points and are clear about the scoring, the set-up (three times), the tapping sequence with reminder phrase (three times) and then rescoring, you'll become very quick indeed. Even now, you are ready to begin using EFT on any riding anxieties and you may find that you'll use it on all sorts of other issues too.

Soon you'll have experience of how fast your body can respond. Whether you work on a traumatic experience that happened many years ago or yesterday, you'll know what it feels like to have an electromagnetic shift in your body. You'll feel your stress level recede as your levels of adrenalin and cortisol drop and your sympathetic nervous system calms down. You now have tool that allows you to release 'stuck' energy and give you emotional freedom.

How to use EFT for rider performance anxiety

The basic EFT recipe that you have already learned is extremely effective for working on your own performance anxiety; you may have to make a few trips through this in order to cover all aspects of your anxiety. Be aware that EFT achieves a much better result the more specific you are so, although you may feel a little calmer about competing after using a very general set-up phrase, using detailed and specific ones can rid you of a problem completely.

An example of the use of a general or 'global' set-up phrase would be to think about how you feel when you are competing and give a score out of 10 as to how affected you are. Your general phrase would be something like *'Even though I'm really nervous when I'm competing, I truly and deeply accept myself'*.

Say this out aloud three times whilst tapping the karate chop point on your hand continuously. Now tap points 1-8 about seven times each and say your reminder phrase: *'feel nervous competing'* at each one. Repeat twice more and then, after a deep breath, reassess your score. You must tune in to the problem by thinking of yourself competing to know if you feel slightly better.

You'll then need to do subsequent rounds in order to reduce your emotional intensity further. Remember that in further rounds we adjust the set-up phrase to: *'Even though I feel some nervousness when I'm competing, I deeply and completely accept myself.'*

Repeat the tapping sequence three times with your reminder phrase and reassess your score.

After a few rounds, you may feel calmer about going out to compete. If it has made little or no difference it's because you haven't been specific. As a practitioner I would avoid such general set-up phrases but the above is all good practice when you are learning the mechanics of it all.

So how can we be specific? Performance anxiety can involve several aspects and it is important that all of them are neutralised using the basic recipe, which may take a few sessions. Just a few minutes a day can be sufficient so don't feel daunted. You need to make a list of exactly what bothers you when you go to a competition, for example:

Fear of falling off

Fear of being out of control

Fear of looking silly

Fear of being watched

Being worried about people thinking your horse is too good for you

Fear of forgetting the test

Being worried by the sound of the bell

Anxious when (horse's name) starts to show the whites of his eyes …

Anxious about flowerpots, music, banners or flags

You then simply treat each of these as though it is an individual problem, for example give yourself a score out of 10 as to how much the fear of falling off worries you. Your set-up phrase would be: *'Even though I'm scared of falling off at a competition, I truly and deeply accept myself.'*

Follow the usual recipe now and tap on points 1–8, repeating a reminder phrase *'scared of falling'* at each point. When you've repeated the tapping sequence twice more, take a deep breath, exhale slowly, tune in to being out competing and reassess your score.

Now repeat subsequent rounds until you achieve as low a score as possible. In principle it would be zero, but even getting down to 2 would indicate a noticeable cognitive shift and the benefits would be significant. This will only have taken you 5 or 10 minutes and may well be enough for one day. In your next session, you can go through the second aspect in the same way, until you have neutralised them all.

Suggested set-up phrases:

'Even though I'm really frightened of being out of control, I truly and deeply accept myself'.
Reminder phrase – *'out of control'*

'Even though I'm worried about looking silly, I …'
Reminder phrase – *'looking silly'*

'Even though I hate being watched, I … '
Reminder phrase – *'hate being watched'*

'Even though I worry that people will think my horse is too good for me, I …'
Reminder phrase *'horse too good for me'*

'Even though I'm frightened of forgetting the test, I …'
Reminder phrase – *'forgetting the test'*

'Even though I panic/feel sick/stop breathing when the bell rings, I …
Reminder phrase – *'panic when bell rings'*

'Even though I panic/feel sick/tense up when (horse's name) starts showing the whites of his eyes, I …'
Reminder phrase – *'whites of his eyes'*

Even though I panic/feel sick/tense up at the flowerpots/music/banners/flags, I …'
Reminder phrase – *'panic at the flowerpots'*

There is often something else to work on. It can be useful to make a list of the physical symptoms you experience when you compete and apply the basic recipe to them too, for example:

'Even though my heart is pounding, I …'

'Even though I feel sick when I enter the arena, I …'

On the day of the competition, and before you get on, you can tap points 1–8 a few times without using any words and whilst you are breathing into your diaphragm. Perhaps you'll be in your stable, lorry or trailer. If you are already in an anxious state, remember, no words are necessary. Just tap and allow the tapping to eliminate the 'zzzzzzt' as Gary Craig describes it. You'll feel noticeably calmer then as you mount, which is always a good start for you and your horse.

If you are in public and you are unable to tap all the points, just tap either on your collarbone point or the karate chop point on your hand. Do this continuously for 2 or 3 minutes. This is a short-cut, emergency tapping technique which can be done surreptitiously and, again, no words are necessary.

Using EFT on the memory of an accident/bad experience

Now that you are practised in a applying the set-up and tapping sequence, or basic recipe of EFT, you'll find it much easier to work with it on other riding-related problems. Many of us have suffered an accident or bad experience and, no matter what we do, the memory and the replayed images seem to haunt present rides. Remember what was said earlier about imagination; our subconscious mind is unable to differentiate between what is real and what isn't. It will understand any thought or image present in that moment as real and your body will respond accordingly.

When we have a traumatic experience like this, it causes a disturbance in our energy system and you'll find that when the blocked energy is released, although you can remember what happened, of course, it no longer has a detrimental effect on you.

Case study

'As a married mother of three children I have been aware of how my thoughts can drift to "what if this happens" and "what if that happens" while I am riding my horses. Having experienced a very frightening prize-giving during the spring of 2012 at the Winter Dressage Championships with my dressage horse, on qualifying for the Summer Dressage Championships my thoughts were already racing – "what if this and what if that …?"

This unscheduled ballet performance was terrifying for the rider, despite the fact that fortunately she and her horse did not part company.

Below: Using EFT tools, she was able to put the memories of this frightening incident aside and enjoy her next championship competition.

I had first met Jane during my Equipilates™ Teacher Training course with Lindsay Wilcox-Reid earlier in 2012 and was most impressed with the introduction Jane gave us to EFT. Little did I realise then just how valuable this would be to me later on. With only four weeks preparation time before the summer championships I booked myself in with Jane and can only describe her taking me through the stages of my previous issues and dealing with them with EFT, as a life-changing experience. I had no idea that, on arriving at the championships only a matter of weeks later, I would be able to use the tools that Jane had given me and cope with the situations that I was faced with. The result was a very happy horse and rider.'

To apply EFT to a traumatic memory, recall it and apply the basic recipe to each part of the memory that causes emotional intensity. It is possible to be rid of the problems it has caused in minutes and in most cases it will never return. So, think of your accident or bad experience as a movie that you are going to play, in very slow motion, in your mind – almost as though you can see each still frame. Narrate the movie out loud in great detail, beginning when everything was okay on your ride and you felt safe.

In your mind's eye, insert your traumatic movie frame by frame.

As you tell it in detail, as soon as you feel any emotional intensity, stop, freeze-frame the picture and apply the basic recipe as though this is a separate traumatic memory. In fact, that is what it is, but it is just part of a larger movie. Perhaps your accident was a bolt on a hack and your ride perhaps began happily when you were walking through woods in a group, but suddenly your horse's (we'll call him Sam) back came up and he grew to 18 hands. When you play your slow-motion movie, this may well be the first time you feel any anxiety – maybe butterflies or a sick feeling in your stomach. This is the picture you freeze-frame and keep in mind whilst you apply the basic recipe that you are now familiar with.

Assess out of 10 how anxious you felt at that point. Your set-up phrase would be: '*Even though I feel sick in my stomach as Sam's back comes up, I …*'

Remember to tap the karate chop point continuously as you repeat this three times. Your reminder phrase would be '*Sam's back comes up*' which you would repeat at points 1–8 while you tap on them. Take deep breath in, exhale slowly, and whilst tuning-in to what was happening in the frozen picture, reassess the score. Repeat this process until you can reduce the score as much as possible; 0 is ideal but 2 or below will make a huge difference to you. Remember that in rounds after the first, you adjust the set-up phrase:

'*Even though I still feel some sickness as Sam's back comes up, I …*'

You then begin narrating your story once again from the beginning and you will notice that, as you come to this point this time, there is little or no emotional intensity; you are aiming for none. You can now continue with the movie – stopping, freeze-framing and applying the basic recipe to every single thing that caused emotional intensity.

Maybe the next freeze-frame would be when Sam was already on the alert, a gun went off in the distance, or a pheasant flew out from the hedge:

'*Even though the gun has gone off and I am panicking, I ….*' Your reminder phrase would be '*the gun has gone off*'.

Each time, go back and narrate your story from the beginning until you can tell it without feeling anxiety. If you do feel any, it is a sign that you do need to stop and apply the recipe to that particular frame once again. Lindsay suffered considerable emotional stress and anxiety after the sudden death of her young horse Taba, who suffered an aortic valve rupture in the field, which she witnessed. After galloping around playing with his sister, he stopped, fell backwards to the floor in distress, managed to struggle to his feet and scramble in a crab-like fashion across the paddock before he crashed into a five-bar gate. He never got up and died in her arms just a couple of minutes later. I used this freeze-frame technique with her some months after the event as it was still extremely traumatic and even a brief memory of the event would bring tears to her eyes. Each little part of the sequence leading up to his death required neutralising and, after our session, she was able to retell the story without emotional intensity.

Depending on what your particular story is, you may have to freeze-frame and tap several times – there are usually peaks or crescendos of emotional intensity that need attention. Once you have dealt with these, you'll feel a huge relief and will certainly notice a difference next time you ride. On occasions, a problem can be complex and in such cases a practitioner would be quicker and more able to find the core issue or cause and treat it accordingly for you.

EFT can do so much more, but my allocated space is full! Do experiment with it and, interestingly, you do not have to believe in the technique for it to work. Even in the hands of relatively proficient newcomers the basic recipe of EFT produces very effective results about 80% of the time and particularly when applied to negative events in one's life.

Happy tapping!

Conclusion

T hank you for joining me on the *Core Connection* journey – I really hope you have found the exercises, techniques and ideas within these pages useful and thought-provoking. You can find out more information about the Equipilates™ coaching, workshops and clinics I offer, together with CPD (Continual Professional Development) courses for riding instructors who may be searching for effective, empowering and ethical teaching tools, plus training opportunities for those wishing to become registered teachers of my approach at www.equipilates.com.

You have a powerful motivator to inspire you to develop and improve as a partner and rider: your horse. If you ever feel that you need reminding why you put so much time, effort, money and emotional energy into this pastime we call equitation, simply look into his eyes and re-ignite the passion in your soul!

Appendix

The Basic 1-2-3 of Emotional Freedom Technique

1. Say what is bothering you. Is it a fear, a memory or something else? Be as detailed as you can. Give a score out of 10 (10 being 100%) as to how much anxiety or emotional intensity it causes you.

2. Say your set-up phrase three times out loud and tap on the karate chop point on your hand:

   'Even though … (describe your problem here) … I truly and deeply accept myself.'

3. Using two fingers, tap on the eight acupressure points shown and say your reminder phrase about the problem. Or you can just say 'this problem' to focus your attention.

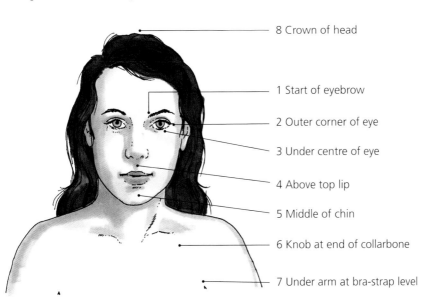

The karate chop point

8 Crown of head

1 Start of eyebrow

2 Outer corner of eye

3 Under centre of eye

4 Above top lip

5 Middle of chin

6 Knob at end of collarbone

7 Under arm at bra-strap level

The EFT tapping points.

Now take a deep breath into your diaphragm and exhale slowly. Close your eyes for a few seconds and tune into your problem. Has anything changed? Reassess your score. Repeat the 1-2-3 process on the remainder of the problem or other aspects of it.

The 1-2-3 process is fully described in the Mind Matters chapter.

(Jane Reid www.mindmatters-ripley.co.uk)

Recommended Reading

Publications

Beck-Broichsitter, Johannes, *Lateral Work: Training for a Supple Horse*, Cadmos Equestrian, 2009

Craig, Gary, *The EFT Manual*, Energy Psychology Press, 2008

Gronberg, Pauli, *ABC of the Horse, Anatomy, Biomechanics, Conditioning*, Pg Team Oy, 2002

Harris, Susan, *Horse Gaits, Balance and Movement*, John Wiley & Sons (new edn), 2005

Heuschmann, Dr Gerd, *Tug of War*, J.A. Allen, 2007

Hilberger, Oliver, *Schooling Exercises in Hand: Working Towards Suppleness and Confidence*, Cadmos Equestrian, 2009

Karl, Philippe, *Twisted Truths of Modern Dressage*, Cadmos Equestrian, 2008

McLean, Andrew and Paul McGreevy, *Equitation Science*, Wiley-Blackwell, 2010

Palmer, Sue, *Horse Massage for Horse Owners: Improve Your Horse's Health and Wellbeing*, J.A. Allen, 2012

Schuthof-Lesmeister, Ellen and Kip Mistral, *Horse Training In-hand: A Modern Guide to Working from the Ground Work on the Longe, Long Lines, Long and Short Reins*, J.A. Allen, 2009

Wilcox-Reid, Lindsay, *Pilates for Riders*, J.A. Allen 2010

Websites and other resources

www.acpat.org (Association of Chartered Physiotherapy in Animal Therapy)

www.blackcountrysaddles.com (For more information on saddles featured in this book)

www.blissbedding.com (Horse bedding suppliers to the Dressage Studio horses)

www.emofree.com and www.eftuniverse.com (Information on Emotional Freedom Technique)

www.equipilates.com (More information on Lindsay Wilcox-Reid's tuition and teacher training courses)

www.equitationscience.com (Not-for-profit organisation aiming to facilitate research into the training and welfare of horses)

www.equitationscience.co.uk (The home of equitation science in the UK)

www.ITSmovesUK.com (Information about Intelligent Training Systems and how to find a Biomechanics Coach)

www.mastersaddlers.co.uk (The Society of Master Saddlers)

www.matchydressage.com (Suppliers of all colour co-ordinated horse clothing in this book)

www.mindmatters-ripley.co.uk (Information on EFT for riders)

www.saddleryservices.co.uk (Advice on saddle fitting)

Index